PORTAL
to the CORPS

PORTAL

Chronicling the National Museum of the Marine Corps

to the CORPS

Edited by Jessica del Pilar

images
Publishing

Published in Australia in 2007 by
The Images Publishing Group Pty Ltd
ABN 89 059 734 431
6 Bastow Place, Mulgrave, Victoria 3170, Australia
Tel: +61 3 9561 5544 Fax: +61 3 9561 4860
books@imagespublishing.com
www.imagespublishing.com

Copyright © The Images Publishing Group Pty Ltd 2007
The Images Publishing Group Reference Number: 747

National Library of Australia Cataloguing-in-Publication entry:

del Pilar, Jessica H.
Portal to the corps: chronicling the National Museum of the Marine Corps.

ISBN 9781864702095 (hbk.).

1. National Museum of the Marine Corps. 2. Fentress Architects (Firm).
3. Military museums – United States – Design and construction.
4. Military museums – United States – Design and plans.
5. Museum architecture – United States – Designs and construction.
6. Museum architecture – United States – Designs and plans. 7. Museum architecture.
I. Title.

727.6

Coordinating editor: Robyn Beaver

Designed by The Graphic Image Studio Pty Ltd, Mulgrave, Australia
www.tgis.com.au

Digital production by Splitting Image Colour Studio Pty Ltd, Australia
Printed by Everbest Printing Co. Ltd., in Hong Kong/China

IMAGES has included on its website a page for special notices in relation to this
and our other publications. Please visit www.imagespublishing.com.

Contents

ENTWINED

in the history of our great Nation is the storied legacy of the United States Marines. For 231 years, the raw physical courage, rigorous discipline, and iron will of Marines on and off the battlefield have earned a reputation that is second to none. This heritage is sacred to our Corps, and not since the dedication of the Marine Corps War Memorial in 1954 has there been as tangible a tribute to the United States Marine Corps' legacy as the founding of the National Museum of the Marine Corps.

The design of this museum reflects the crest of Mount Suribachi on the island of Iwo Jima, where in the closing months of World War II the image of five Marines and one Sailor raising the American flag was seared into our national consciousness.

Foreword

General Michael W. Hagee, 33rd Commandant of the Marine Corps

Sixty years has done little to diminish the striking images of Iwo Jima. This hallmark battle is one link in the long chain that binds all Marines together—from the Continental Marines at Bunker Hill to the *Teufelhunden* crossing the wheat fields of Belleau Wood, where in 1918 they stemmed the tide of battle after being told that the war was lost. This chain binds us to the Marines on Guadalcanal in the early days of World War II, whose fighting spirit and unshakable determination prevailed over disease, privation, and relentless enemy attacks from the land, sea, and air. It passes through the ice and snow of the Chosin Reservoir, through the steaming jungles of Vietnam, and is anchored firmly in the current battlefields of the Global War on Terror.

Preserving this history means a great deal to Marines; our history is the standard against which we measure our performance today. We study the great Marines who fought in our touchstone battles and analyze what they did to forge the modern Marine Corps. Marines serving today stand in awe of the accomplishments of previous generations who fought and sacrificed for the United States around the globe. They gladly shoulder the responsibility to uphold the legacy they have inherited.

The National Museum of the Marine Corps is a place for every Marine—both past and present—to reflect on our heritage and pay tribute to the Marines of yesteryear. It is also a place where we commemorate the service and honor the memory of each of our fallen. Most of all, it is a place where we will tell the Marine Corps story to all Americans—and it's a great story to tell.

Semper Fi

Mike Hagee

01:

G THE MARINES AT THE FRONT,
ORGANIZATION IN THE WORLD."

GENERAL DOUGLAS MACARTHUR, US ARMY

"THE SAFEST
PLATOON OF M

Esprit de Corps

Colonel Joseph H. Alexander, USMC (Ret)

IN KOREA WAS RIGHT BEH

ES. LORD, HOW THEY COUL

MAJOR GENERAL FRANK E.

AMERICA

established a corps of Marines even before the nation declared its independence from Great Britain. Created on November 10, 1775 by the Continental Congress, the Marines have literally grown up with the nation; an intrepid band of sea soldiers committed from the start to preserving their country's freedom. Within weeks of their creation, the new Marines boarded ships of the Continental Navy, eluded the British blockade, and captured an enemy fort in the Bahamas, the first of their storied flag raisings around the world.

Photos and quotes representative of all Marines line Leatherneck Gallery.

Proficient on land or sea, and inherently useful during emergencies, the Marines have acquired a unique eyewitness view of historical events. Marines crossed the Delaware River with George Washington; raided the British homeland with John Paul Jones; marched 600 miles across the Libyan desert in the attempt to free US hostages held captive in Tripoli; stood with Andrew Jackson against British regulars at New Orleans; sailed with the Wilkes Expedition to discover Antarctica; stormed Chapultepec Castle, "The Halls of Montezuma," in Mexico City; rescued the hostages held by John Brown at Harpers Ferry; accompanied President Lincoln to Gettysburg for his haunting address; and stopped the German advance on Paris in World War I after three weeks of horrific fighting at Belleau Wood.

Armed with little more than Springfield "03" bolt-action rifles and their bold new doctrine of amphibious assault, the Marines launched the Pacific War's first offensive by landing on Guadalcanal in 1942; later they stormed the heavily defended bastions of Tarawa and Iwo Jima, vital stepping stones to Tokyo. In the first winter of the Korean War, the First Marine Division fought its way through ten Chinese divisions from "Frozen Chosin," or the Changjin Reservoir, to the sea.

Traditional Marine readiness and their unrelenting forward presence in troubled waters helped the nation persevere throughout the 40-year Cold War with the Soviet Union. Yet, as Secretary of the Navy Edwin Denby observed in 1921, "There is no peace for Marines." Subsequent peacekeeping and counterinsurgency operations in Lebanon, Somalia, Afghanistan, and Iraq took a frustrating toll in casualties and public support, but also spurred the Marines' adaptations to the changing nature of 21st-century warfare.

Patrons are given the unique opportunity to experience these and other remarkable stories through the architecture and exhibitory of the National Museum of the Marine Corps, which was guided by the following core statement and nine primary messages.

Core statement

The Marine Corps provides a vital contribution to the nation and the preservation of freedom.

Primary messages

1. Marines are a global, expeditionary force-in-readiness. The Marine Corps has unfailingly provided the nation with ready forces; forces that are armed and equipped for sustained, short-notice deployment with fleets around the world. Their ageless slogan: "First to Fight," is less a chest-thumping boast of past achievements than an operational goal for the immediate future. Evidence of this professional readiness appeared as early as the Creek and Seminole Wars of the 1830s, when the Commandant closed his Washington office to lead half the Corps in the field. The Marines deployed ready forces with the first wave of U.S. troops to France in World War I; to Iceland, Samoa, and Guadalcanal as World War II began; and to Pusan and Inchon in the first desperate months of the Korean War. A reinforced Marine division rapidly converged on Da Nang as the first air-ground combat troops to deploy to Vietnam in 1965. An entire Marine Expeditionary Force, 80,000-strong, deployed on short notice to Saudi Arabia in 1990, fully armed and organized for sustained combat in the liberation of Kuwait.

2. Marines operate in partnership with the U.S. Navy—and have since 1775. Operating closely with the Navy fleet allows Marine expeditionary forces to reap the benefits of mobility, surprise, and access provided by the open seas. This unique seagoing teamwork began early in the Revolutionary War with the landing on New Providence. And as recently as 2001, helicopter-borne Marines launched from Navy amphibious ships in the Arabian Sea for an unprecedented 400-mile deployment into Afghanistan. In addition to enabling forcible entries across hostile shores, this historic Navy–Marine relationship bears a number of other benefits. Navy chaplains, doctors, dentists, and hospital corpsmen have served in the ranks of Marine field units in every campaign over the last century. Twenty-three of these individuals have received the Medal of Honor for their commitment under fire "above and beyond the call of duty."

3. Marines fight as a self-sufficient, combined-arms team—ground forces, aviation, and logistics support in a single task force. Marine Air–Ground Task Forces provide the national command authority and joint combatant commanders with useful, flexible forces in any crisis—fully integrated task forces that train together, arrive early, and are ready to fight. Marines have been an air–ground team since the dawn of military aviation. One of every four Marines serves in an aviation unit. Marine pilots provide responsive close air support to their fellow Marines on the ground. Other aviators serve as forward air controllers with infantry units. Integrated firepower from aircraft, naval gunfire, and field artillery protects Marine maneuver forces as they storm ashore.

4. Tough training and shared hardships forge the Marines' warrior spirit. Marines are warriors by choice and temperament; they are ingrained with an aggressive spirit and a willingness to engage the enemy at close range. Rigorous basic training instills discipline, initiative, and teamwork in new recruits and officer candidates. Marines learn to thrive on chaos, a consequence of being "First to Fight." Earlier Marines were described as "shock troops." Combat correspondent Robert Sherrod modified that label after sharing the Marine landings at Tarawa, Saipan, and Iwo Jima. "They're not shock troops," Sherrod wrote, "they're *shock-proof* troops."

5. Every Marine, air or ground, is a rifleman. Marines take pride in their marksmanship. John Thomason wrote of the "Old Breed" Marines arriving in France in 1917: "Rifles were high and holy things to them." A year later the same Marines cut down German infantrymen with well-aimed fire from 800 yards at Les Mares Farm near Belleau Wood. Other armed services provide an obligatory weapons familiarization for their non-combatant specialists. The Marines have no non-combatants. Every Marine—officer or enlisted, regular or reserve, man or woman, pilot or "grunt"—must be proficient with their assigned weapon. This distinctive axiom has paid enormous dividends: the Marine artillerymen picking up their carbines to withstand the Japanese *banzai* attack at Saipan, the Marine truck drivers wielding their M-1s against ambushing Chinese Communists near Koto-ri, North Korea, and the Marine cooks taking up arms against North Vietnamese infiltrators at the Liberty Bridge combat base in Vietnam.

6. The Marines' traditions of rapid deployment and assault from the sea demand constant innovation. Marines must innovate to survive. Rapid, global deployment and amphibious assaults, two of the most difficult military operations, require Marines to be constantly innovative in doctrine, force structure, weapons, and tactics. Marine innovations led to the doctrine for forcible amphibious assault; the doctrine of extremely close air support to ground troops; the tactical employment of helicopters; the air–ground, combined arms task force; the doctrine for fighting "Small Wars;" the use of Navajo code talkers; the Combined Action Program in

counterinsurgency wars; the concept of forward-based maritime pre-positioning as a strategic mobility enhancement initiative; the pre-deployment qualification of entire expeditionary units as "Special Operations Capable;" long-range tilt-rotor aircraft; and the "three-block war" concept of 21st-century urban warfare.

7. For Marines, uncommon valor is always a common virtue. Careful planning, violent execution, and quick-witted adaptation characterize expeditionary operations and amphibious warfare. Examples abound: Presley O'Bannon crossing the Libyan Desert in 1805; the fleet Marines storming Fort Sumter in a long-shot night attack in 1863; the 5th and 6th Marines advancing through the wheat toward Belleau Wood; the former stunt pilot Christian Schilt landing his biplane in the streets of Quilali, Nicaragua, to evacuate wounded Marines; the 2nd Marine Division attacking across the reef at Tarawa; Gregory "Pappy" Boyington, the leading Marine fighter ace, challenging Japanese pilots at Rabaul to come up and fight his "Black Sheep" squadron; the Marines of Fox Company defending Toktong Pass at "Frozen Chosin;" the 1st Marine Division's wild tank battle in the Burquan Oil Field in 1991; and the protracted urban battle for Fallujah in Al Anbar Province, Iraq in 2004.

8. Marines instill leadership by example in all ranks. Like any armed force, the Corps reveres its legendary combat leaders, such as Chesty Puller, Joe Foss, Merritt Edson, and Ray Davis, but the distinctive story of the Corps concerns the legions of lesser-known Marines who swallowed hard and stepped up to take the lead when the plan went awry or their commander went down. Examples include Sergeant John Quick in the assault of the Sohoton Cliffs in the Philippines; Gunnery Sergeant Dan Daly at Belleau Wood; Staff Sergeant Jimmie Howard's defense of Hill 488 in South

Vietnam; Corporal Charles Ingraham, directing airstrikes from his rooftop in Khafji, Kuwait, while surrounded by Iraqi soldiers; Sergeant James Wright retaining command of his ambushed squad in Iraq despite losing both arms to a rocket-propelled grenade.

9. The Marine motto *"Semper Fidelis"* (always faithful) epitomizes the virtues of honor, courage, and commitment. *Semper Fidelis,* the Marines' motto since 1883, has evolved into a special bond, an affirmation, and a work ethic. In essence it means that Marines take care of their own, including the recovery of their dead and wounded comrades—no matter what it takes. The motto also means there are no "ex-Marines." Membership is for life.

In conveying these primary messages to visitors, the National Museum of the Marine Corps offers a combination of artifacts, images, testimonials, audiovisual presentations, interactive displays, dioramas, full-scale tableaus, oral histories, maps, and immersion galleries.

The crown jewel of the artifacts is the U.S. flag raised by the Marines on the crest of Mount Suribachi on the fourth day of the battle for Iwo Jima, the scene captured in Joe Rosenthal's Pulitzer Prize-winning photograph. The smaller first flag, raised under enemy fire several hours earlier, is displayed alongside.

Two dozen Marine aircraft are suspended overhead, ranging from fabric-covered biplanes to attack jets and helicopters. Full-sized tableaus on the floor of the Central Gallery capture the moment of the Marines' first use of "Alligator" tracked amphibians in the assault on Tarawa in 1943, and the first use of transport helicopters to deliver infantry troops into battle at Hill 884 in Korea, 1951.

Other large artifacts catch the eye, including tanks, assault amphibians, howitzers—even the unique and much-maligned "ONTOS," a pint-sized tracked vehicle sporting six 106mm recoilless rifles. Many macro artifacts are displayed within a realistic tableau. The "Alligator" amphibian is jammed across a Japanese seawall, a Sherman medium tank approaches an enemy cave at Peleliu, the ONTOS guards a shell-swept intersection in the 1968 battle for Hue City.

All weapons used by the Marines and many others captured from their enemies are displayed. Some Marine weapons reflect their traditional propensity for closing with the enemy—boarding axes, pikes, and cutlasses in olden days; submachine guns, portable flame throwers, and K-Bar fighting knives in more modern times. Several tethered weapons, breeches safely sealed, give visitors the heft and feel of such classic firearms as the Garand M1 rifle, the Browning Automatic Rifle, and the Vietnam-era M79 40mm grenade launcher.

Intermixed with the weapons displays are artifacts of a less lethal nature, such as bandmaster John Philip Sousa's original sheet music for his march *Semper Fidelis,* and an authentic 18th-century leather stock, worn by the earliest Marines to protect their necks from enemy cutlass slashes in ship-to-ship fighting (hence the abiding nickname *Leathernecks).*

Full-scale "Marine Life" exhibits capture the Marine experience at various points in history. All Marine recruits and officer candidates stood "Junk on the Bunk" inspections, laying out their clothing and equipment on top of their bunks for the commanding officer's critical eye. A World War II tableau captures such a scene at Montford Point, the segregated recruit depot in North Carolina that prepared the first African-American volunteers for service as U.S. Marines.

Immersion galleries portray the Marines' experience during three touchstone battles: D-Day at Iwo Jima, 1945; the defense of Toktong Pass by Fox Company 7th Marines during the Chosin Reservoir campaign in North Korea, 1950; and the defense of Hill 881 South, the critical outpost protecting the besieged Marine base at Khe Sanh, South Vietnam, 1968.

Visitors at the Iwo Jima exhibit "ride" an assault craft to Green Beach on D-Day, surrounded by actual footage and sounds of the ship-to-shore assault into the teeth of Japanese defenses. When visitors enter Toktong Pass the temperature drops, the Siberian winds hit, and the lights fade to depict a Chinese night attack against the nearly frozen defenders of the critical pass. In Vietnam, visitors "ride" a CH-46 Sea Knight helicopter to the hilltop, debarking quickly to avoid the inevitable mortar fire from nearby North Vietnamese gunners.

For all its illustrious artifacts, the National Museum of the Marine Corps places greater emphasis on the faces, stories, and accomplishments of its people. A number of "Individual Marine" displays introduce visitors to Leathernecks of all ranks and achievements. Among those highlighted are legendary World War II figures like Col Lewis ("Chesty") Puller, Gunnery Sergeant "Manila John" Basilone, the raider LtCol Evans Carlson, and LtGen Roy Geiger, the first Marine and the only aviator of any service to command a field army in battle. Among the Korean War Marines are Capt Robert Barrow, a future Commandant whose rifle company spearheaded the recapture of Seoul, MajGen Gerald Thomas, a division commander who served as a sergeant at Belleau Wood and Soissons in World War I, and Capt Ted Williams, the future Hall of Fame baseball player with the Boston Red Sox, who flew combat missions in an F9F Panther jet. Vietnam-era individuals include Navy Chaplain

Vincent Capodanno, whose protection of wounded Marines under fire resulted in a posthumous Medal of Honor, and PFC Charles Mawhinney, the sniper with a Corps-best 103 confirmed kills.

Museum visitors can listen to 30 recorded oral histories from individuals who served from Guadalcanal through the 1968 Tet Offensive in Vietnam. World War II testimonies include one of the storied Navajo Code Talkers, a sergeant in Edson's Raiders, and a former Congressman who as a child witnessed the liberation of his native Guam by the Marines. Korean War testimonies include a motor transport officer who helped rescue hundreds of survivors of Task Force Faith from the ice of Chosin Reservoir, and an enlisted Marine pilot, shot down, captured, and imprisoned by the North Koreans. Vietnam-era oral histories include that of the Marines' first black aviator, a fighter squadron commander who would become the Corps' first black general, a helicopter crew-chief shot down four times during medevac missions, and the survivors of a reconnaissance patrol ambushed above Dong Ha.

The personal words of hundreds of other Marines are displayed to visitors, sometimes in letters home from distant battlefields and more often as direct quotations that introduce each exhibit panel.

Audiovisual programs educate visitors throughout the museum, beginning with an introductory series of testimonies by 16 men and women in the Orientation Theater. Visitors can stand on the famous "yellow footprints" at Boot Camp as anxious recruits arrive to begin their transformational process or step into a unique kiosk to experience a personal "guidance" session with a very attentive Drill Instructor. Alcove theaters along the Fast Track Gallery provide audiovisual examples of the Marines' distinctive warfighting methods—launching "from the sea" to force entry to inland objectives, deploying and fighting as an integrated air–ground team, relying on innovation and field improvisation to achieve tactical advantages. Another Fast Track exhibit invites visitors to browse the life stories and citations of all Marines and attached Navy and Coast Guard personnel who have received the Medal of Honor. A similar exhibit offers an interactive search for all Commandants and Sergeants Major of the Marine Corps. A flight simulator challenges visitors to experience a combat mission as "pilot" or "gunner" in a modern jet fighter.

The Marine Corps Heritage Foundation provided the vision and leadership to create the national museum. The late Col Gerald C. Thomas, Jr. USMC (Ret) personified the Foundation's dedication to this multi-year project.

The other principal leaders in the NMMC project have contributed chapters to this book. All of the Marine authors served in combat in the Republic of Vietnam. Generals Hagee, Christmas, and McKay, and Col Ripley were all company commanders. Colonel Long was then an enlisted radio operator, typically the "most valuable player" in any firefight. All contributed their experience and leadership to the design of the museum and its exhibits.

Other retired officers contributed significantly to the vision and design of the National Museum storyline, including Gen Carl E. Mundy, the 30th Commandant, and BGen Edward H. Simmons, Director Emeritus of Marine Corps History.

The membership of the exhibit design team changed over the five-year effort, but among those who contributed significantly were Brian Chaffee, project architect for Fentress Architects; Col Jon Hoffman, LtCol Robert Sullivan, Ken Smith-Christmas, Charles Girbovan, Keith Alexander, Charles Grow, and Beth Crumley of the former History and Museums Division of Headquarters, Marine Corps; Christopher Chadbourne, Peter Barton, David Whitemyer, William Ruggieri, Mary Macfarlane, Julie Duncan, Robert Krick, and Kimberly Nelson-Hanser of Christopher Chadbourne and Associates; and Robin Sylvestri, Alice Rubin, James Lovell, and Tara O'Boyle of Batwin and Robin Productions. Collectively, their contributions helped illuminated the Marines' ongoing story, a history that renews itself each new day in some far-off corner of the earth.

Colonel Alexander, author of *Utmost Savagery: The Three Days of Tarawa*, served as lead historian for the NMMC exhibit design team from 2001 through 2006.

02:

At 210 feet tall, the National Museum of the
Marine Corps is visible to passersby along
Interstate 95.

A Monumental Project

Lieutenant General Ronald Christmas, USMC (Ret)

WHILE most Americans know something about the U.S. Marine Corps, most don't know what it actually means to be a Marine. That's where this Museum differs from other military museums: every decision we've made is driven by our wish to share the experience of life as a U.S. Marine, its monumental challenges and unparalleled rewards.

In 1999, the Marine Corps Heritage Foundation and the United States Marine Corps partnered to create a monumental National Museum. For the Foundation—a small nonprofit institution founded in 1979 to research and chronicle the Marine Corps' historic contributions to the nation—the mission appeared challenging. Among the many vital considerations were:

- What would be the Museum's primary mission?
- What types of exhibitions and programs would best carry out this mission?
- Where should the Museum be located?
- How much would it cost and where would the money come from?
- How could we ensure that the new facility would be world class in all respects, and fittingly take its place among this nation's historical treasures?

Defining the vision

Our first priority was to assess and establish a compelling vision. This vision evolved from discussions with historians, educators, museum professionals, individual Marines, and the senior leadership of the Marine Corps.

Early on, we recognized the need for the National Museum to be responsive to the hopes and dreams of Marine veterans. Veterans ardently believe the lessons and values made incarnate by Marine Corps service have educational value to non-Marines. These lessons and values, garnered over several centuries, embrace the qualities of industry, energy, integrity, determination, enthusiasm, justice, self-discipline, sacrifice, honor, courage, and commitment. Therefore, we realized our story needed to be told "through the eyes of Marines"—a theme that became the title of our principal fundraising case statement.

We also began to perceive the National Museum as a centerpiece for the Marine Corps Heritage Center. The Center, envisioned as a mecca for Marines and their families as well as a place of learning and respect for all Americans, was master planned to include a memorial park, conference facilities, Marine association offices, and even overnight accommodations.

In short, our vision led us to embark on a grand project for the nation.

Thinking about exhibitions

Concurrent with developing our vision, we sought to define our exhibitory goals. We wanted to employ multiple types of exhibits to adequately communicate our history— Revolutionary War to the present—as well as allow room to document future events. We looked at a wide spectrum of exhibit types—from those that could be understood quickly to others that required an extended time commitment in order to be fully appreciated. With such a lengthy and diverse history, it was difficult to choose which types would be used to depict which eras and epochs.

Eventually, we determined the Museum would comprise an orientation theater, an experiential boot camp exhibit, and several major explorative galleries tied together by a fast-track corridor. The theater and boot camp would orient visitors to our mission of seeing "through the eyes of Marines." The modular gallery and fast-track corridor would allow us to pre- and post-date our opening-day exhibits with additional epochs and eras.

Location and design

We were fortunate early on to have Prince William County, home to Marine Corps Base Quantico, offer us an attractive, 135-acre parcel of land flanked by Interstate 95 and the main entrance to Quantico. A study conducted through George Mason University found this location to be an attractive venue, capable of drawing residents and school children from the Greater Washington metropolitan area, as well as national and international tourists.

Proximity to Interstate 95 would also afford the Museum considerable visibility from the thousands of vehicular passengers that traverse this section of highway each day.

Meeting the financial challenge

When we undertook the task to create this monumental Museum, the total financial commitment to bring the Museum and Heritage Center to fruition was unclear.

Estimates ranged from as low as $20 million to as high as $100 million.

While total cost was vague, the division of responsibility between the Marine Corps and the Heritage Foundation was straightforward. The Marine Corps would fund infrastructure development, exhibit planning, and ongoing operations. The Foundation would fund construction, by way of private donations, and then, upon completion, gift the facilities to the Marine Corps.

The Founders' Wall recognizes significant contributions made by donors to the Museum.

**Craftsmen engrave Founders' Wall in
Leatherneck Gallery.**

In keeping with Marine tradition, opportunities and risks were assessed and a strategy was designed to win the fundraising battle ahead. The line of departure was crossed and the rest—a great deal of hard, demanding work requiring determination, teamwork, organization, and creativity— is history.

More than 80,000 devoted Marines responded to a direct-mail campaign and therein became members. This gave us the momentum and resources necessary to develop our campaign. Additionally, more than 100 Founders—comprised primarily of successful Marine veterans—endorsed the project and made significant financial commitments. They also spearheaded solicitations to fellow Marines, foundations, corporations, and friends who shared their vision of the Museum and Heritage Center.

Every step of the way, these Founders offered the Foundation not only philanthropy, contacts, and business capabilities, but also their ideas, encouragement, and passion for success.

The original capital campaign collected more than $60 million to open the first phases of the Museum and Semper Fidelis Memorial Park. More remains to be done on this journey to complete the full Heritage Center, replete with a memorial park, walking trails, chapel, and a variety of other amenities and attractions.

Making of a national treasure

For the Museum's architecture, we elected to carefully orchestrate a national design competition. We felt this was the best means to find and select an architectural firm with the creative prowess necessary to design this national treasure. From the more than 30 submissions of interest, we selected four firms to compete. Fentress Architects emerged as the winner. The firm's design was a striking representation of our culture and mission: the semblance of Rosenthal's picture of the flag raising on Iwo Jima and many other onward, at-the-ready, strong, iconic Marine Corps images. Fentress Architects' experience worldwide on cultural and civic institutions only served to bolster what we perceived as the most significant design submitted.

The National Museum of the Marine Corps is truly a monumental project for the United States of America. The tremendous effort to develop this newest national treasure not only demonstrates the ethos of America's Marine Corps, but also the country as a whole.

03:

The Competition

Colonel Joseph C. Long USMCR (Ret)

"WE are a Corps born of an act of Congress, consecrated in sacrifice, steeped in tradition and tested in battle," stated Gen J.L. Jones at the United States Marine Corps' birthday celebration in 2001. While Gen Jones and his fellow Leathernecks genuinely understand what it means to be a Marine, few non-Marines fully fathom the experience.

And yet, in the summer of 2000, four architectural firms were asked to not only understand, but also interpret the Marine Corps experience in a comprehensive design. These firms were finalists in the national design competition for the United States Marine Corps Heritage Center and its National Museum of the Marine Corps.

Rosenthal's photo overlaid on a section of the Museum helps convey Fentress' design inspiration.

Laying the groundwork

The Marine Corps Heritage Foundation
had a two-part call to action in the mid-
1990s with Congress' passage of legislation
encouraging each branch of the military to
create a national museum, and continued
frustration with the substandard housing
of the Corps' more than 60,000 priceless
artifacts. The Foundation sketched out
an idea for a campus with a world-class
Museum and state-of-the-art curatorial
facilities. In 1997 this conceptual campus,
which would become known as the Marine
Corps Heritage Center, was presented to
Commandant and Gen Chuck Krulak. He
liked it. In fact, he elected to support the
idea by forming an Executive Steering
Committee (ESC) to be chaired by the
Assistant Commandant.

One of the first courses of action undertaken
by the ESC was the initiation of an
Environmental Impact Study in 1998. The
original goal of the study was to determine
the best of three sites; all of which were
located on Marine Corps Base Quantico
at the direction of Gen Krulak. However,
during the public comment period a fourth,
and what would become the most desirable
site, emerged. The Prince William County
Park Authority offered 135 acres of
undeveloped, wooded land that was flanked
by the Base's front gate and Interstate 95.
Ownership of this land was transferred to
the Department of the Navy at a public
ceremony in September 2001.

Meanwhile, the ESC was also working with
the Foundation to commission preliminary
master plan and programming studies for
use in the design competition. The firms who
performed these studies were the Prentice
Company of Chicago, the Onyx Group of
Alexandria, Virginia, and the Washington,
DC office of Douglas-Gallagher. Collectively,
their recommendation was to create the
United States Marine Corps Heritage Center:
a conference hotel, a 1500-seat auditorium,
a memorial park, large artifact restoration
and storage buildings, a parade ground, a
demonstration area, Marine Corps-related
office buildings; and most significantly, a
premier museum capable of accommodating
half a million visitors annually.

The museum was further defined. With all
phases complete, it would be a structure of
some 200,000 square feet, including 60,000
square feet of exhibit space, a giant-screen
theater, restaurant, gift shop, offices,
computer research lab, extensive combat
art curatorial and display area, and
classrooms. The exhibit area would utilize
a "hub and spoke" arrangement whereby
visitors could spend most of their time
in only the era galleries that were of most
interest to them. It would also have a boot
camp, Officer Candidate School gallery,
and orientation theater.

The design competition

With the master plan and program established, the Marine Corps moved forward with a design competition on November 30, 2000. Working through the Department of the Navy's Engineering Field Activity Chesapeake (EFAChes), commanded by Capt William Boudra, a multi-stage national competition was announced. Project Manager for EFAChes, Tess Manns, and I, the Heritage Center Program Manager for the Marine Corps, oversaw the process.

The first stage, which required applicants to submit their qualifications, drew almost thirty architects. As Ms. Manns recalls, "It was interesting. Even though the competition was only open for a short time during the holidays, we had some of the top architects in the country respond."

In the second stage, a Technical Panel composed of Col Gerald Thomas (Ret) of the Marine Corps Heritage Foundation; LtCol Jon Hoffman, Deputy Director of the Marine Corps' History and Museums Division; and Bob Greco, Tess Manns, and Tracey Johnson from EFAChes, narrowed the list to four firms: Fentress Architects; Hellmuth, Obata + Kassabaum (HOK); Tuck Hinton Architects; and Leo A. Daly. Each was given an honorarium of $50,000 and six weeks to develop a preliminary design and prepare a model depicting their building design and site plan. Additionally, representatives of all four firms were invited for a site visit. At one point during that visit, I stopped the group and showed them on the map that Interstate 95 turns just before it reaches one of the site's high points. I suggested that if they were to design the building for this location, northbound traffic would have it directly in their line of sight. And if their design were dramatic enough, traffic reporters would refer to it in the same way they talk about traffic backing up to the Mormon Temple on Washington DC's Beltway.

For the third phase of the competition, two days were set aside during which each architectural team gave a three-hour presentation to a single audience composed of two groups. The first group was a jury of architects: Richard Logan, Vice President at Gensler; Gregory Hunt, Dean of Architecture at Catholic University; Eric Van Aukee, Vice President at Perkins + Will; and Hal Aber, Director of Design and Planning for the Smithsonian. This group made a recommendation to the second group, the Selection Board, which ultimately chose and presented the winning firm to the Commandant of the Marine Corps for final approval.

Fentress Architects' competition boards illustrating inspiration and planning concepts.

Fentress Architects emerged as the winner with a design defined by a signature mast. The mast, which soars at a 60-degree angle from the floor of the central gallery through a 160-foot-tall atrium, is evocative of many aspects of Marine Corps life. Most notably, it reflects the Joe Rosenthal photograph of the second raising of an American flag atop Mt. Suribachi on the island of Iwo Jima during World War II. A longer contemplative look will also evoke a rifle with bayonet attached, a Howitzer firing at high angle, or a jet aircraft taking off, among many other images.

The design presentations were conducted at the Washington Navy Yard. All four firms had done an incredible amount of due diligence, which was evident in the detailed models, and unique ideas presented.

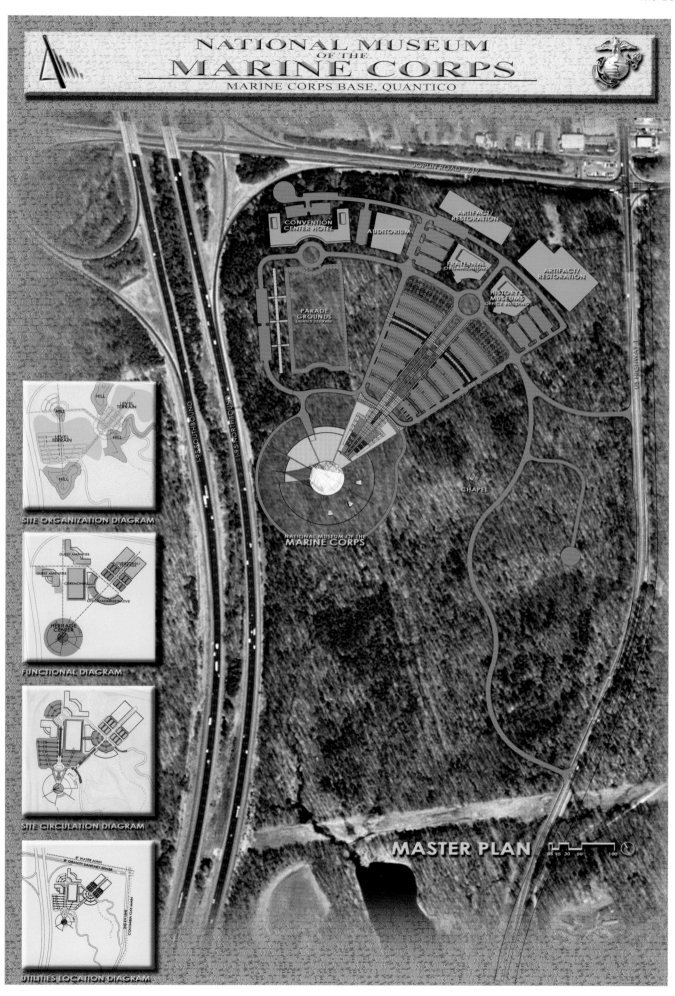

NATIONAL MUSEUM
OF THE
MARINE CORPS
MARINE CORPS BASE, QUANTICO

SITE ORGANIZATION DIAGRAM

FUNCTIONAL DIAGRAM

SITE CIRCULATION DIAGRAM

UTILITIES LOCATION DIAGRAM

MASTER PLAN

Fentress Architects' competition boards
illustrating elevations and first floor plan concepts.

Members of the Selection Board included Gen Joseph Went (Ret), LtGen Ron Christmas (Ret), and Marsh Carter, all of the Foundation; Col John Ripley (Ret), Director of the Marine Corps' History and Museums Division; and Tony Diagonale, William Faught, and Maggie Gervais, each head of a division of EFAChes. Fentress Architects was the first presenter, and therefore in the difficult position of having to be especially memorable. And it was.

With LtGen Christmas and Col Ripley, I presented the Fentress Architects' design to Gen James Jones, then-Commandant of the Marine Corps. Gen Jones quickly agreed that it was an impressive design and signed the appropriate form. Then he stated, "We need to green it up a little." The non-Marine translation: ensure both the architect and exhibit designers are thoroughly immersed in Marine Corps history and culture to guarantee the design reflects a personal knowledge and understanding of the United States Marine Corps. In ensuing months numerous trips were made by the architectural and exhibit designers to Marine Corps training bases and battle sites.

Gen Jones' selection of Fentress Architects to design the National Museum of the Marine Corps was made public on July 9, 2001. We were really glad we did a design competition. I never realized how great this process could be.

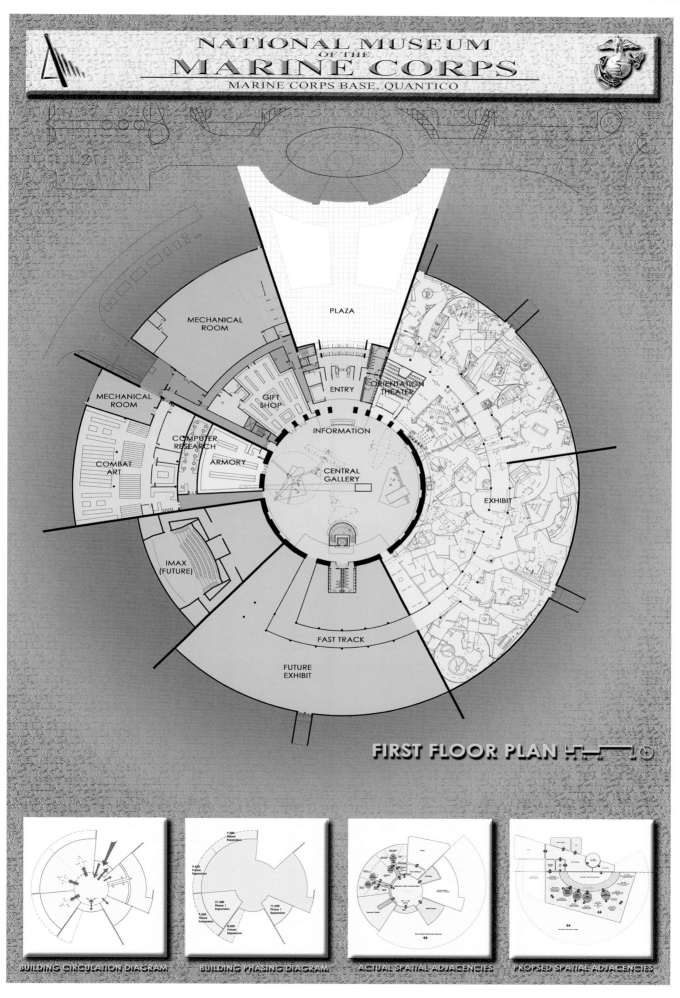

NATIONAL MUSEUM
OF THE
MARINE CORPS
MARINE CORPS BASE, QUANTICO

PLAZA

MECHANICAL ROOM

MECHANICAL ROOM

GIFT SHOP

ENTRY

ORIENTATION THEATER

INFORMATION

COMPUTER RESEARCH

ARMORY

COMBAT ART

CENTRAL GALLERY

EXHIBIT

IMAX (FUTURE)

FAST TRACK

FUTURE EXHIBIT

FIRST FLOOR PLAN

BUILDING CIRCULATION DIAGRAM

BUILDING PHASING DIAGRAM

ACTUAL SPATIAL ADJACENCIES

PROPSED SPATIAL ADJACENCIES

28

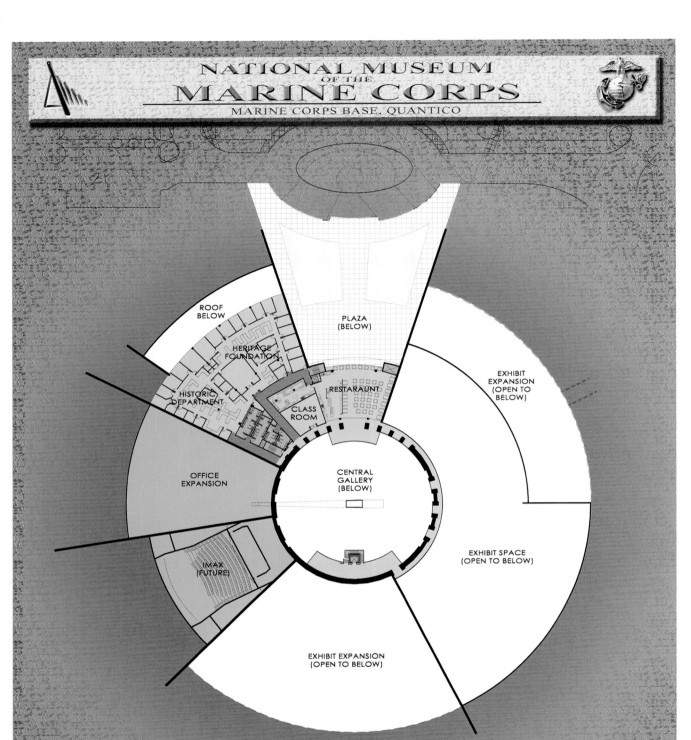

NATIONAL MUSEUM
OF THE
MARINE CORPS
MARINE CORPS BASE, QUANTICO

ROOF BELOW

PLAZA (BELOW)

HERITAGE FOUNDATION

RESTARAUNT

HISTORIC DEPARTMENT

CLASS ROOM

EXHIBIT EXPANSION (OPEN TO BELOW)

OFFICE EXPANSION

CENTRAL GALLERY (BELOW)

EXHIBIT SPACE (OPEN TO BELOW)

IMAX (FUTURE)

EXHIBIT EXPANSION (OPEN TO BELOW)

SECOND FLOOR PLAN

UNITED STATES MARINE CORPS HERITAGE CENTER AREA CALCULATIONS		
	120K Plan	Proposed
HD & HF office suites	12,000	12,473
Armory (display)	3,500	3,513
Classroom	2,000	1,971
Restaurant	4,500	4,500
Bookstore	5,000	5,119
Reception Area	5,000	2,645
Exhibit space	60,000	60,075
Triage/Loading Dock/Area	1,500	2,013
Combat Art	13,000	13,112
Heritage Research Area	1,500	1,596
Other miscellaneous space	12,000	
Toilet Rooms		2,900
Info/Security/Costs/Strollers/etc		664
Docent Lounge		243
Vertical Circulation		2,337
General Circulation		9,906
Service Areas		2,134
Mechanical Equip Room		3,389
Total	120,000	128,590

ENTRY PLAZA | WELCOME | CELEBRATION OF THE INDIVIDUAL MARINE | KITCHEN

TERRACE

SECTION PERSPECTIVE

Fentress Architects' winning entry

To contrast with the sharp upswept point of the soaring mast, Fentress Architects buried much of the Museum in a hill on one of the site's highest points. This approach not only proved to be more sustainable, but also more horizontal in nature than those of the other finalists.

The central gallery, housed in an atrium, enshrouds the mast and defines the building's organization and form. Visitors enter through a guest services lobby and then into this dramatic space where displays of Marines and their equipment honor the individuals who serve the United States Marines Corps.

Fentress Architects' competition boards illustrating inrerior rendering and sustainability concepts.

The southern portion of the site was preserved for the demonstration grounds and the Semper Fidelis Park. This park features both a memorial chapel and an outdoor exhibit illustrating the development of amphibious landings.

"The question we kept asking ourselves when designing this center was, 'What is it to be a Marine?'" said Curtis Worth Fentress, Principal-in-Charge of Design at Fentress Architects, when asked to comment on his team's design process.

Initial inspiration came from the sense of strength evoked by the flag raisers at Iwo Jima. It was the Japanese attack on Pearl Harbor on December 7, 1941, that shocked the world and brought the United States into World War II. By 1945, the Marine Corps was in the midst of one of the most demanding and brutal battles in the history of its organization. The battle of Iwo Jima went on for almost a month, during which 71,000 Marines fought to overcome the defenders. Over 6,000 Marines died and more than 17,000 were wounded in battle. Iwo Jima not only marked the turning point to victory in the war, but the Rosenthal

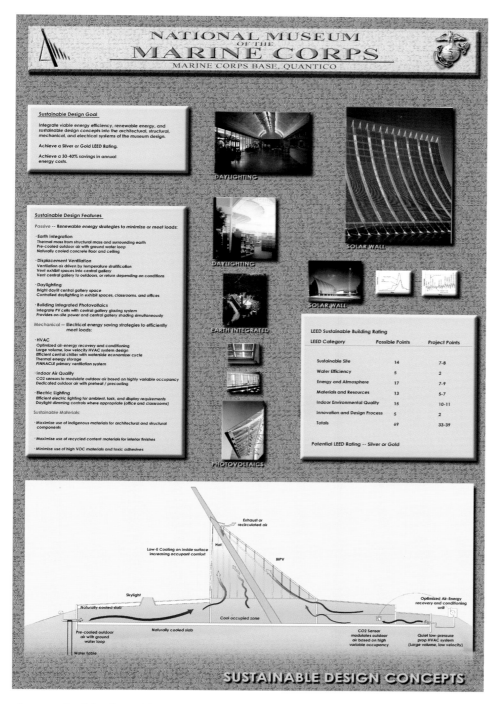

photograph of the flag raising atop Mt. Suribachi became one of the most recognized and enduring symbols of the United States Marine Corps. The Corps' War Memorial, which is in itself a replica of that event, provided further inspiration with its inscription by Fleet Admiral Chester W. Nimitz: "Uncommon Valor was a Common Virtue."

This inspiration evolved into a soaring 210-foot mast that recalls more than simply the flag raisers; it evokes notions of swords at salute, Howitzers ready for fire, upward and onward images of powerful aircraft take-offs, bayoneted rifles held in advance and drawn swords at their apogee. This dramatic composition of structural lines creates a poised image of strength and stability as it interprets the spirit of the Marine Corps.

From the southbound approach road, visitors experience increasingly dramatic views of the Museum between trees. At night, these views become picturesque as the building sits bathed in moonlight on the hill.

Other finalists' entries
Hellmuth, Obata + Kassabaum (HOK) entry

The HOK design is fluid. Its white fabric roof, suspended with a cable system, sets the tone for the mellifluous qualities that are carried throughout. Access to the museum is gained by crossing a long pier-like structure that spans an enlarged lake area. Once past the lake, the fabric roof's open-air courtyard shelters patrons and mediates between the museum and future components, such as an IMAX theater.

The museum's entry is a two-story atrium, which provides access to the exhibit and gallery spaces lying beneath the courtyard. Administrative and support facilities are located in a bunker-like structure that is carved into the back of the museum. Dramatic night lighting and the flag that waves proudly above this structure are open symbols of homage to the United States and its Marine Corps.

Partial collection of HOK's competition materials.

SOUTH ELEVATION

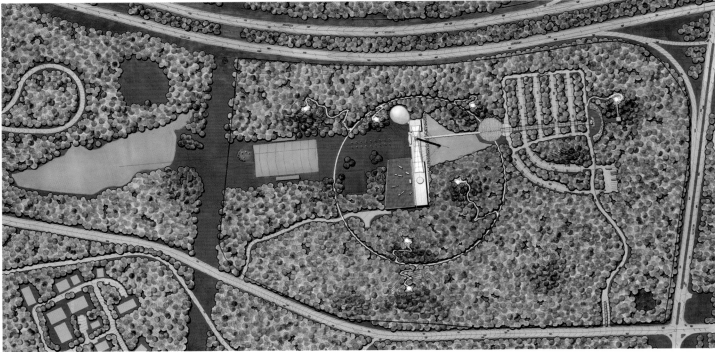

SECTION A-A

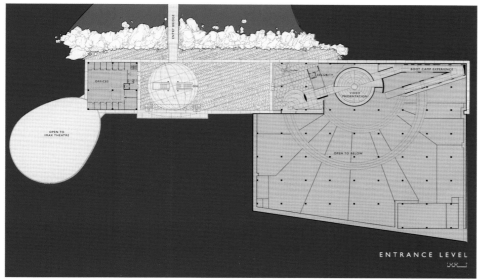

ENTRANCE LEVEL

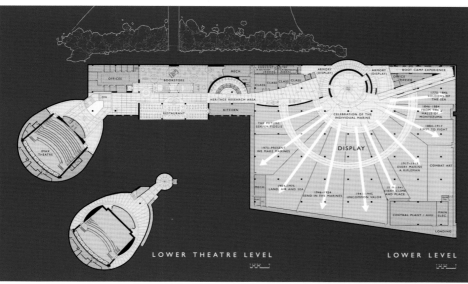

LOWER THEATRE LEVEL   LOWER LEVEL

Tuck Hinton entry

The Tuck Hinton team began with comprehensive placement of major elements and features. The site's composition is geometrical—all elements radiate on an axis from the middle of three hills on the site. The pathway that connects these three hills is in celebration of "Honor, Courage and Commitment."

The entrance to the museum lies at a 45-degree angle from the middle hill. The building's entrance, façade, and a portion of its roof are demarcated with an abstraction of bayonets and swords. These strong, spear-like elements were inspired by, among other images, the Marine Corps' swords at salute.

The museum's location near an interstate highway offers maximum visibility. As viewed from the interstate, the building is designed to portray a straightforward, simple, protected, "of-the-earth" appearance. In concert with these ideas, the approach road offers views to a very simple three-story linear façade, which is anchored by a circular drop-off zone and a circular theater complex. Housed within the linear portion are the exhibit and gallery spaces. Amphibious vehicles and tanks are located on the lower level, while the split upper levels house suspended and grounded aircraft.

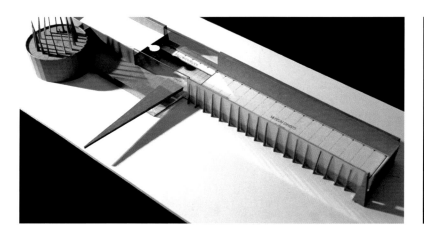

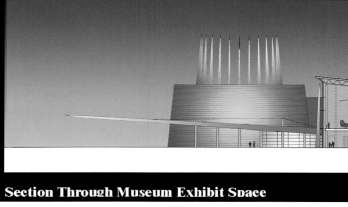

Section Through Museum Exhibit Space

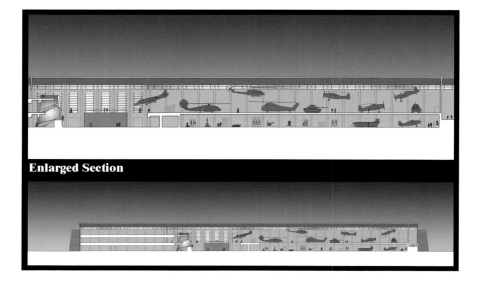

Enlarged Section

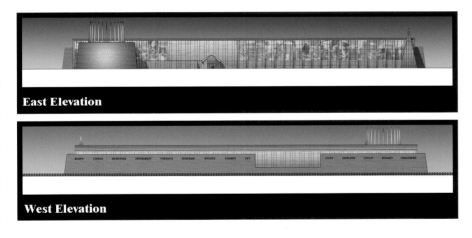

East Elevation

West Elevation

Partial collection of Tuck Hinton's competition materials.

Leo A. Daly entry

Leo A. Daly's design is sensitive to the site's natural features. The entrance to the Heritage Center is located very close to the north campus, where the visitor experience begins. A monument announcing the museum and a small water feature are integrally designed. As visitors reach the tree clearing, they are greeted by a view of the museum across a series of three reflecting pools. Continuing along this roadway, past the parade grounds, three stone pylons with the inscription "Honor," "Courage," and "Commitment" greet visitors. As visitors travel down the entrance drive toward the building, they view an embossed emblem of the Marine Corps. From here, the entrance is clearly identified with soaring panels of stone and a curtainwall façade over the entrance doors.

The design relies on the beauty of efficiency, directness, and poetry. Efficiency is seen in the simplicity of two bars set side-by-side and in the structural clarity of the design. Directness is seen in clearly marked building circulation systems, which link all the museum's parts in a simple sequence of spaces. The poetry of the design is illuminated in the intuitive symbolism of individual components within an overall composition.

Partial collection of Leo A. Daly's competition materials.

Competition finalist descriptions are reproduced from "Documenting Pride: A US Marine Corps Heritage Center in Virginia" by Jessica H. Sommers, Competitions *12, No 2, 2002, pp 6–15.*

04:

THE Marine Corps is a proud organization with its own distinctive ethos, history, customs, courtesies, and way of doing business. It is organized in self-contained Marine Air–Ground Task Force systems; each task force, regardless of size, includes command, air, ground, and support elements. Marines train to be offensive in nature. They take seriously the Marines' Hymn line "First to Fight," and they pride themselves on being ready at a moment's notice. They are inspired by aggressive action. "Send in the Marines," "Tell THAT to the Marines," and "The Marines have landed and the situation is well in hand" are phrases often quoted with personal satisfaction.

Marine Commandant Gen James Jones recognized that the designers of the National Museum of the Marine Corps must understand these subtleties of the Corps, so he gave instructions for the designers to be "greened up." Fentress Architects had already captured the Corps' attention and goodwill with their competition-winning design. Now they would continue to refine it, inside and out. And, significantly, they would be managing the contract for the exhibit design firm, Christopher Chadbourne Associates of Boston.

Exhibits in Leatherneck and the other galleries depict Marines in action.

Greening the Team

Colonel Joseph C. Long USMCR (Ret)

Bootcamp

Design team members Brian Chaffee of Fentress Architects and Chris Chadbourne and Bill Ruggieri of Christopher Chadbourne Associates arrived at the Receiving Barracks of the Marine Corps Recruit Depot after dark. The team readily complied when encouraged to board a bus with a contingent of new recruits. Amid much shouting, they and the recruits were hustled off the bus and made to stand at attention on the famous yellow footprints; there, new recruits receive their initial instructions on how to stand at the position of attention, how to respond to the Marines in charge of them, and what to do next. The team was told to turn in their personal items, including cell phones, before kneeling on the ground to read a wall plaque of regulations that govern recruit behavior. The entire group was then rushed into a room where they stood in line to receive the clothing and materials needed for training. It was at this point that the design team was extracted from the aggregation of recruits and became observers.

During the ensuing week, the designers observed bedtime, get-up time, close order drill, classroom instruction, and swim qualification. Forty miles north at Camp Pendleton, they stood on a firing line as recruits fired M-16A3 rifles, which helped bring home the adage, "Every Marine a rifleman." Then came the toughest part of bootcamp—*The Crucible*: a 54-hour exercise that represents actual field conditions. During this exercise recruits get little sleep and just two meals a day. The designers watched recruits participate in team building and problem-solving actions, do fire and movement exercises day and night, and finish with a 10-mile forced march. Then came the finale, a warrior's feast to acknowledge the tremendous accomplishments of the recruits.

Left to right: Marines at bootcamp; Project
architect Brian Chaffee at the firing range.

Upon graduation, the recruits earned the right to be counted among "The Few, The Proud, The Marines."

Shipboard life

Marines are a sea service. As such, they are expert at amphibious landings. For the Museum's design team to understand this important element of Marine Corps life, they needed to spend time aboard a ship. Arrangements were made for the same design team that participated in bootcamp to board the USS *Nassau* off the coast of North Carolina. The team was berthed in a junior non-commissioned officer's area in the hold of the ship. One of them proclaimed it "the frat house of the Marine Corps" because of the lack of privacy. With a

Opposite, top and bottom: Marines at bootcamp.

Below, left to right: Design team aboard
USS *Nassau*.

common headroom, also known as a
restroom, there was a certain amount of
towel-popping levity. However, when it
came time for the landing exercise to begin,
the Marines were all business. The designers
were invited to sit in on the Commander's
brief to his staff and subordinate
Commanders. They were then allowed to
enter the amphibious tracked vehicles and
helicopters. And just prior to the landing of
the troops, they flew back to Camp Lejeune
aboard a Marine CH-53 helicopter.

44

Belleau Wood

Many Marine Corps historians accept the World War I battle of Belleau Wood, France, as the single most important event that re-shaped the Marine Corps from a ship-bound organization to the force in readiness it is today. Curtis Worth Fentress of Fentress Architects and Bill Ruggieri of Christopher Chadbourne Associates joined Col John Ripley (Ret), Director of the Marine Corps' History and Museums Division, Col Jerry Thomas (Ret) of the Marine Corps Heritage Foundation, and me for two days of walking the battlefield where, in June 1918, German soldiers had been so strongly positioned they beat back effort after effort to dislodge them. It was a terrible fight, but finally, with the Marines in the vanguard, the battle was won. Ruggieri actually sat in a trench from which a German machinegun would have been firing at Marines attacking across an open wheat field. Based on that point of observation he designed the Belleau Wood immersion experience for the Museum.

Above, left to right: Memorial at Belleau Wood; Pavillon de Chasse; Col John Ripley; Aisne-Marne American cemetery.

Opposite, left to right: Beaches of Iwo Jima; Aerial photograph of Mt. Suribachi on Iwo Jima.

The Pacific Islands

There has never been flesh against steel as there was in the island campaigns of the Pacific Theater during World War II. To help the design team grasp the spirit of the brave men who experienced those horrific battles, Fentress and Ruggieri were taken to Guam, Saipan, Tinian, and Iwo Jima. They stood atop Iwo's Mt. Suribachi where Joe Rosenthal photographed the famous flag raising more than a half century earlier. They walked the black volcanic sands where thousands of Marines had fallen under withering Japanese fire. They traversed deep into the hot bowels of the island's lava crust as they traced the labyrinth of caves still holding furniture made from Japanese ammunition boxes, Saki bottles, and even a rusted old rifle standing in a rifle rack.

These trips were just the beginning. Greening the team became an integral part of the entire process, from initial project meetings through construction completion. The design team emerged from the experience fully enveloped by the Marine Corps nomenclature and regular attendees at some of its most time-honored events.

A significant byproduct of this "greening" process was the sense of team that developed among the Marine Corps, the Marine Corps Heritage Foundation, the architects, and the exhibition designers. Future efforts were simplified and made better because each party more thoroughly understood the others.

05:

President George W. Bush speaks at the
dedication ceremonies on November 10, 2006.

Project of a Lifetime

Curtis Worth Fentress

ANNOUNCED

in November 2000, the architectural competition for the United States Marine Corps Heritage Center coincided with a particularly tumultuous time in recent history—the dotcom crash caused stock markets worldwide to plunge, the USS *Cole* was attacked, the Palestinian/Israeli conflict was escalating, and for the first time ever, the U.S. presidential race was settled by a Supreme Court vote.

As Fentress Architects began preparing its submission, I found myself thinking back to a quote I am often inspired by, but found particularly appropriate in this instance: "In the middle of difficulty lies opportunity" (Albert Einstein). At this tumultuous time, opportunity was exactly what we faced. We were being challenged to create an icon for the country's most elite branch of the military. Moreover, it was to be a landmark, counted among the most significant and historical treasures of greater Washington, DC.

Joe Rosenthal's photograph for the Associated Press captures the flag raising on Mt. Suribachi on the island of Iwo Jima.

The philosophy that has guided Fentress Architects for more than 25 years is *Inspired Design for People*. As opposed to Post-Modernism, Art Deco, and Neo-Classicism, this style does not encapsulate an era in time nor is it dictated by external forces like current trends, fashionable materials, or the promulgation of a predetermined look. Rather, *Inspired Design for People* is informed by the unique combination of elements that define a specific project. An area's history, culture, memory, and myth are examined as sources from which to evoke built forms. Elements of nature and interpretations of cultural and historical references are called upon to produce solutions that operate on metaphor, symbol, and even legend. Taking these abstract concepts from theory to reality is what sharpens architects' skills, feeds their passion for the trade, and ultimately, instills a greater sense of humanity in the built environment.

Gen J.L. Jones stated at a United States Marine Corps' birthday celebration, "We are a Corps born of an act of Congress, consecrated in sacrifice, steeped in tradition and tested in battle." While Gen Jones and his fellow Corpsmen genuinely understand

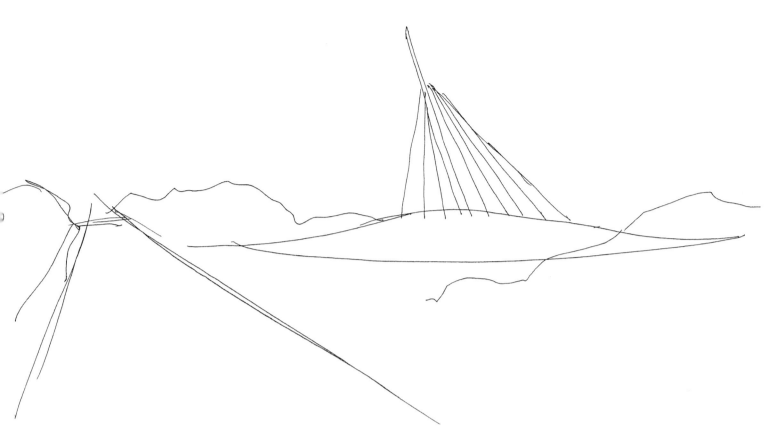

Curtis Worth Fentress' early sketch of how the museum would appear from the Interstate.

what it means to be a Marine, few non-Marines fully fathom the experience; whence came the architectural challenge for this museum: learn what it means to be a Marine.

For the Heritage Center and its National Museum of the Marine Corps, we began the process of discovery, or what we term the "patient search," with questions. First, general ones like:

- What is unique about the United States Marine Corps?
- What is its spirit and what is its culture?

For answers, we immersed ourselves in research—reading every book, watching every video and documentary, and interviewing every Marine, active and retired, that we could find. Initial research yielded an insatiable thirst for knowledge, as the undeniable aura of the Marine Corps and the unparalleled significance of its actions became known to the team.

With research underway, the next step was to articulate symbolic and functional objectives for the Center and its Museum. For each visitor, the design needed to evoke what many Americans already know of their Marines: steadfastness, sacrifice, and integrity. Or, in the words of the Marine Corps Heritage Foundation, the Museum was to "resonate with a child's sense of adventure, a parent's awareness of history and service, and the Marine's sense of Duty and Honor." The Marine Corps has been making history for more than 200 years, and the Center and its Museum needed to bring that history alive in the form of a memorable experience bestowed on each visitor.

50

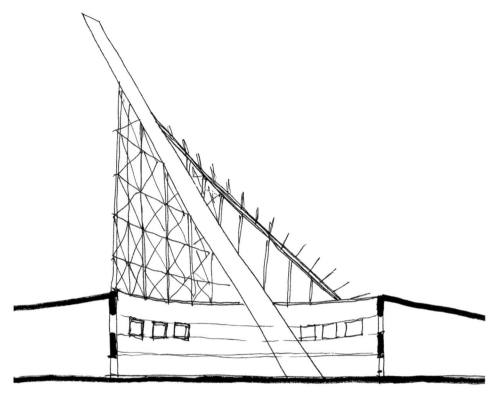

Curtis Worth Fentress' early cross-section sketch illustrating the mast and skylight.

Beyond the symbolic objectives were functional objectives. Marine Corps artifacts had been stored for decades in substandard facilities and had become vulnerable to deterioration beyond repair. The Center and its Museum would correct this by giving these artifacts a permanent, state-of-the-art home capable of contributing to their restoration and preservation. Further, the Center and its Museum were to be accessible, not only to all people on both a physical and mental level, but also to all types of exhibits.

Research and articulation are the necessary foundation for sketches, diagrams, models, and more. The team created hundreds of sketches and many models in search of a form that could be a new Marine Corps icon. That was a tall order to create in a building, but it eventually framed the question, "What image most comes to mind?" History has provided a wealth of battles, beachheads, visual imagery, and colorful personalities in the Marine Corps that could inspire the design to meet the objectives. Of all the rich historical material available, however, the Associated Press image of the flag raisers at Iwo Jima is the most recognized, most enduring symbol of the Marine Corps. Iwo Jima has been referred to as both the turning point battle for victory in the Pacific as well as a defining moment for the future of the Marine Corps.

As we developed the design, I was reminded of the times growing up when my father would discuss World War II. I remember him looking at the famous picture of the flag raising at Iwo Jima. In that moment captured on film, one could discern the excitement and patriotism of those men: the desperate fight, the struggle to take that hill, then the pride of owning the hill.

United States Marines Corps War Memorial in Rosslyn, Virginia near Arlington Cemetery.

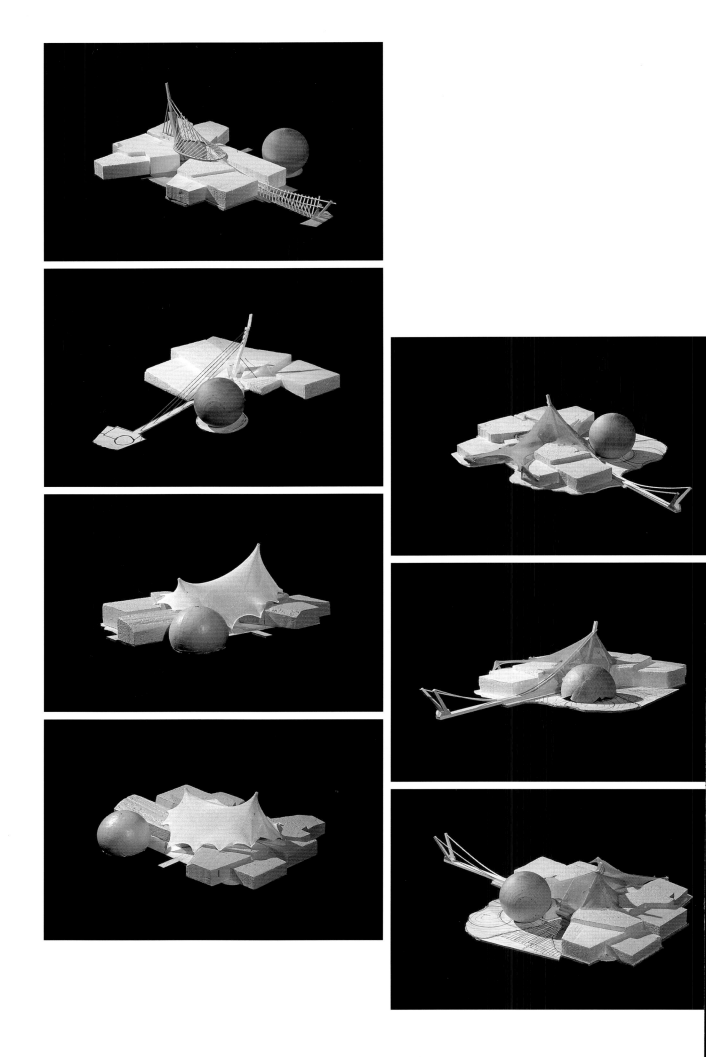

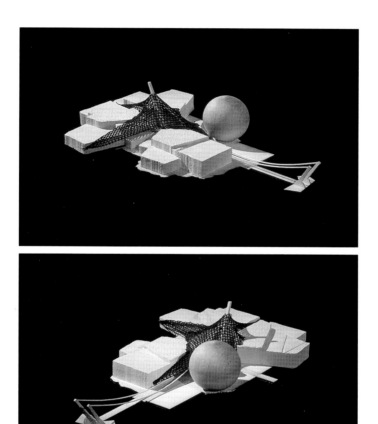

Building concept models from the competition phase.

Site development models from the competition phase.

Marines with bayonets.

While the image of the flag raisers provided the central theme for the building, there are other significant images evident in the signature architectural form that is the Central Gallery. The dramatic upswept point evokes "upward and onward" images of an aircraft's powerful take-off; the bayoneted rifle in the advance; the drawn sword at its apogee; a Howitzer firing at close-range targets, its barrel steeply elevated; the classic etching of the Marine rifleman bursting through the surf and barbed wire at Tarawas (the epitome of "Forward … from the Sea"); the image of exhausted Leathernecks climbing the cargo nets to re-embark their ship after another amphibious assault; or the Marine sharpshooters of the USS *Wasp* scrambling up the rigging to man their "Fighting Tops" in the 1812 battle with HMS *Serapis*. These moments and traditions represent the pride, valor, fidelity, power, readiness, and esprit of the United States Marine Corps. At every progressive stage of design, these values were at the forefront of our minds.

Marines with a Howitzer cannon in Kuwait.

Our sources of inspiration evolved into a soaring 210-foot-tall mast, the signature element that rises at a 60-degree angle through a 160-foot-tall atrium. The atrium is conical in shape and tilted. It is grounded in the earth and at the same time sweeps toward the sky.

Drawing on one of the firm's many strengths, the design team progressed with conceptual model building. As a young architect in New York City, I learned hands-on how models can bring design concepts to life. After all, most clients are not architects and find it challenging to fully comprehend a design in two dimensions.

From initial rudimentary concept models, we progressed into making detailed models of the skylight, central gallery, and staircase. Each model proved extremely valuable in communicating the design intent to our client and getting their feedback as well as identifying the design elements in need of further refinement.

The largest of the models built stood 12 feet tall and was 20 feet long.

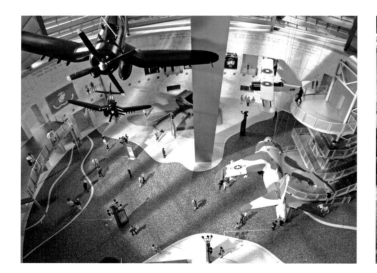

But the largest and most helpful to our clients was a half-inch scale model. It measured 20 feet long by 10 feet wide by 12 feet tall. Through open portals along the first and second level, our clients were able to achieve an eye-level experience. There was even a cut-out in the model's central gallery floor, which when first experienced by Gen McKay reminded him of manning a tank's turret. The viewpoint from this "turret" was what arriving visitors would see.

This model helped determine the exact location for the eagle, globe, and anchor on the mast as well as the quotes and pictures ringing Leatherneck Gallery. It also helped our structural engineers create an even more innovative and cost-effective skylight.

At half-inch scale, this model helped Fentress Architects refine building details and the client to fully fathom the visitor experience.

60

Site model photos illustrating the proximity of
the museum to Interstate 95, the entry road,
and the entrance at night.

Ground broke on the Museum on September 26, 2003 and two short years later, the building opened. Opening weekend festivities coincided with the 231st birthday of the Marine Corps on November 10, 2006. The three-day-long celebration included a formal dedication, at which President George W. Bush spoke, as well as Commandant Michael Hagee and Bill Lehrer.

Above: President Bush (far right) and moderator Jim Lehrer, retired Marine (far left) pray during the opening ceremonies.

Right: US Marine Drum and Bugle Corps play at the preceding evening's gala.

Opposite

Left: Commandant Hagee and Curtis Worth Fentress greet one another at the gala.

Right: Senator, Astronaut, and Retired Marine John H. Glenn, Jr. gives opening remarks at the gala.

For me, the opening was exhilarating. I am, and will forever remain, in awe of Marines. To participate in the creation of a new national treasure is a high point for my career. Looking back on the more than seven years we dedicated to the first phase of this project, the early years seemed to have required a great deal of patience from all parties involved. During that time, our days were filled with resolving an infinite number of details in order to get the project off the ground and in design. We dealt with post-September 11, 2001 changes to building codes, federal budgeting, and economic forecasting for cultural facilities. The design team, inspired by the client, rose to every challenge and brought forth inspired solutions. In contrast to the design phase, construction flew by. Then again, this phase always passes quickly for me; perhaps that is because construction animates a building.

In retrospect, I feel confident we helped the Marine Corps Heritage Foundation achieve the goals set out in the competition: the creation of a shrine, a schoolhouse, and a memorial. The Museum now educates people about Marine Corps history, while providing a place to remember all those who have served. Without a doubt, this building exhibits the greatest degree of permanence of all the projects with which Fentress Architects has been honored.

06:

THE National Museum of the Marine Corps symbolizes the defining moment of the Marine Corps as we know it today: the flag raising at Iwo Jima. This enduring image became the central architectural theme for the 120,000-square-foot museum. Fentress Architects' inspiration evolved into a 210-foot-tall soaring mast sweeping upwards toward the sky. Located under the soaring mast, the 160-foot-tall, glass-enclosed central gallery defines the building's form and organization. Visitors enter through a lobby and then into the dramatic gallery where large exhibits are displayed. Visitors see history through the eyes of the Marines. The site is organized to give its soaring keystone, the Museum, high visibility from adjacent Interstate 95, on which more than 100,000 cars travel each day.

The Museum

THE SITE. The Museum and its site truly complement one another. Generously donated by Price William County, the 135-acre sprawling site has rolling topography and dense forest. Following a survey, it was clear that the Museum would benefit tremendously from being located atop the site's highest peak, which also corresponds with a bend in the Interstate. This bend places both north- and southbound traffic on axis with the Museum. With the mast rising above the tree line, passersby are engaged with the building for several moments at a time. The effect is dramatic. During the day, the stainless steel glistens, while at night the glass is luminous.

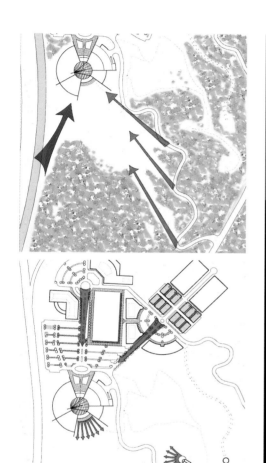

Visitors enter from Route 1 on the east side of the building. The approach road provides access to surface parking for 400 cars. The visitor drop-off area, adjacent to a grand public plaza, is on an axis with the building entry.

The southern portion of the site is preserved for demonstration grounds and the Semper Fidelis Memorial Park.

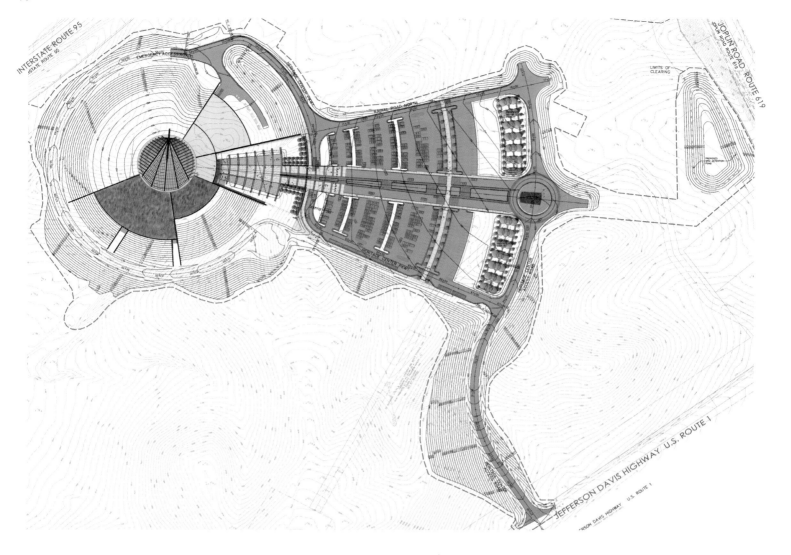

The entry road focuses on the Museum,
its entry, and an entry plaza.

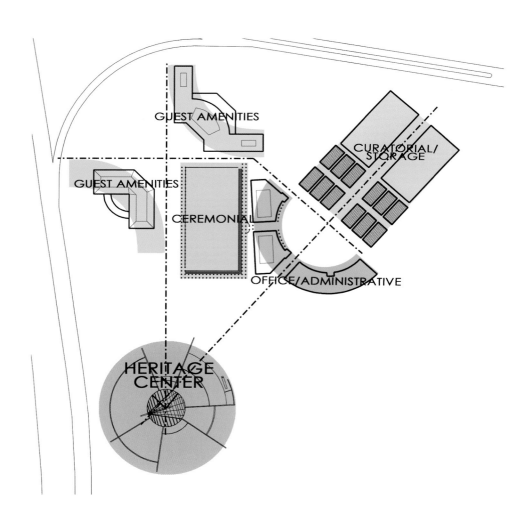

GUEST AMENITIES

GUEST AMENITIES

CURATORIAL/
STORAGE

CEREMONIAL

OFFICE/ADMINISTRATIVE

HERITAGE
CENTER

The building's functions have an axial site organization wherein the curatorial, storage, and administration spaces are along one axis, and public amenities, hotel, and theater spaces are along the other axis. The parade ground and temporary artifact storage anchor the axes.

The most significant distinguishing factor between the original and final master plans is that the final plan is rotated approximately 22 degrees to the west.

This entry road provides access to surface parking areas accommodating 400 cars. A visitor drop-off area adjacent to a grand public plaza leads to the building entry.

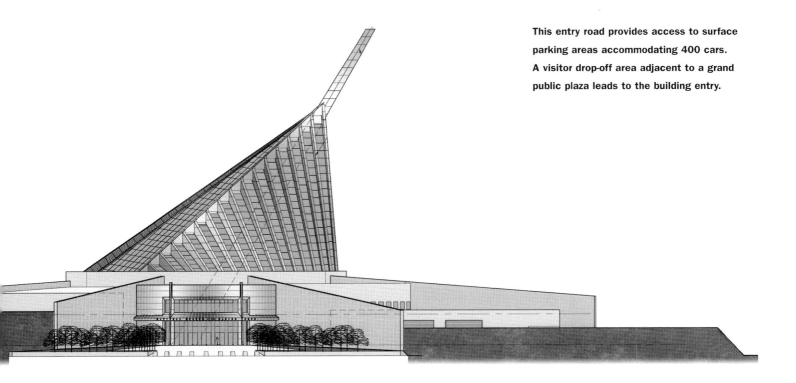

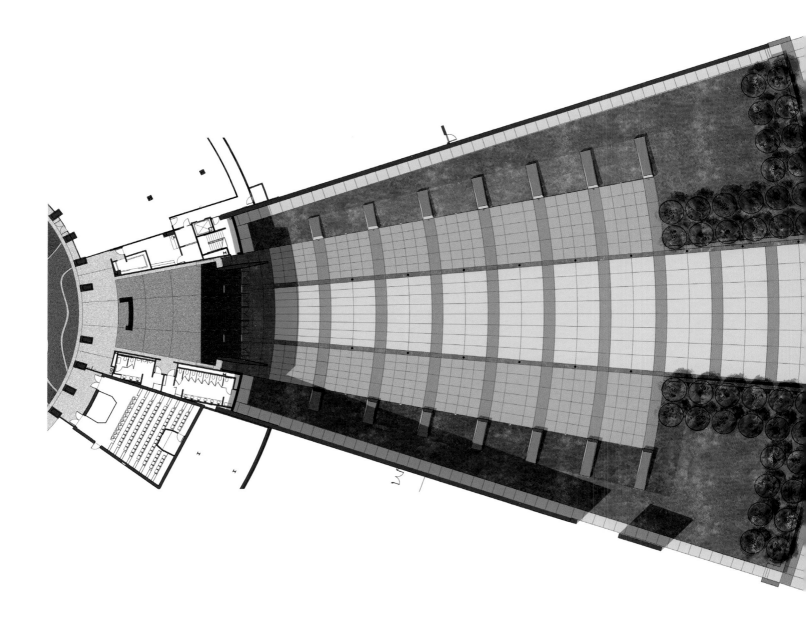

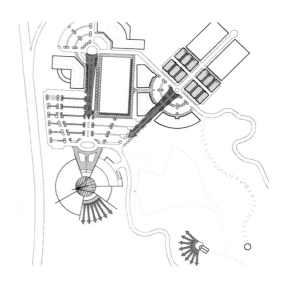

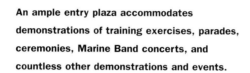

An ample entry plaza accommodates demonstrations of training exercises, parades, ceremonies, Marine Band concerts, and countless other demonstrations and events.

True to Marine form, the museum is composed of modest, yet highly functional building materials, including cast-in-place concrete, metal, and glass. Exterior walls are cast-in-place concrete. They are minimally decorated with a defined-form tie hole pattern and lightly sandblasted to ensure uniformity of color and texture.

From the plaza, visitors enter through doorways distinguished with stainless steel and glass.

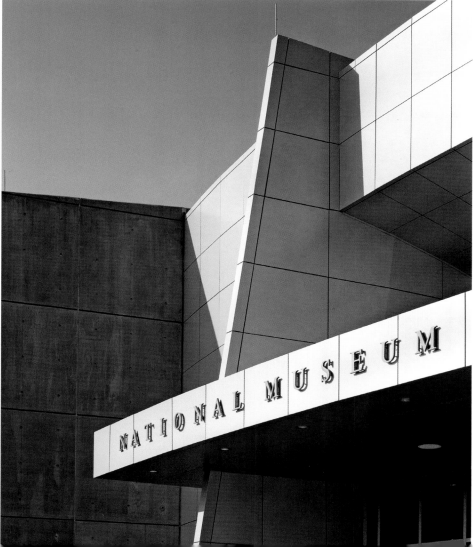

Museum visitors are greeted in a guest services lobby,
which provides orientation services, tours, and access
to ample public restrooms.

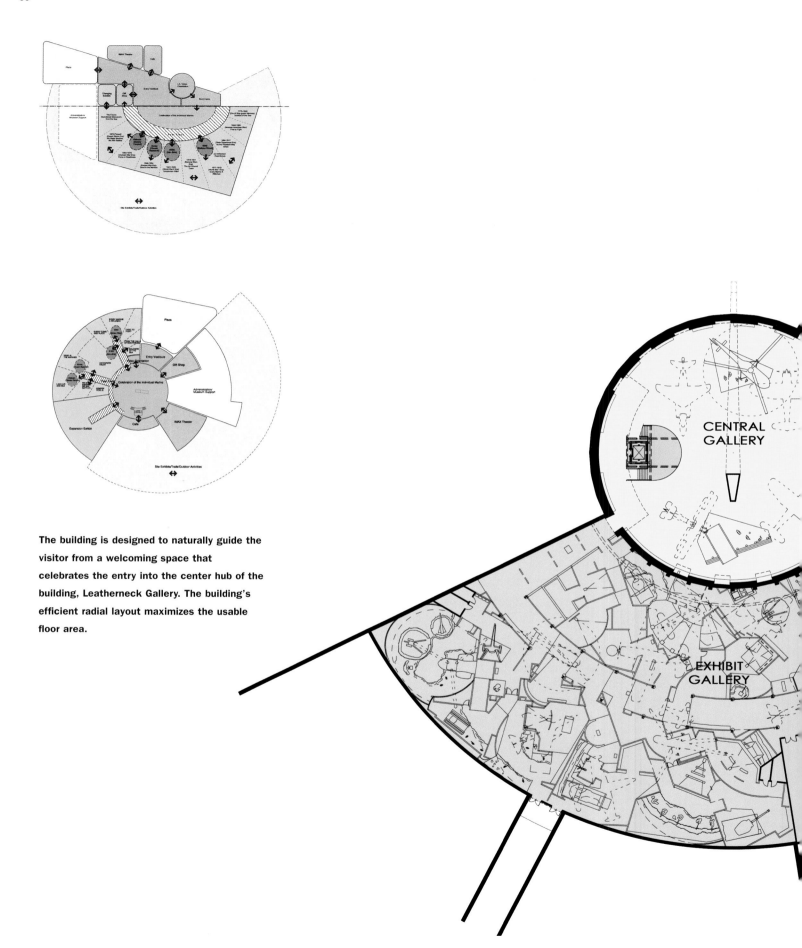

The building is designed to naturally guide the
visitor from a welcoming space that
celebrates the entry into the center hub of the
building, Leatherneck Gallery. The building's
efficient radial layout maximizes the usable
floor area.

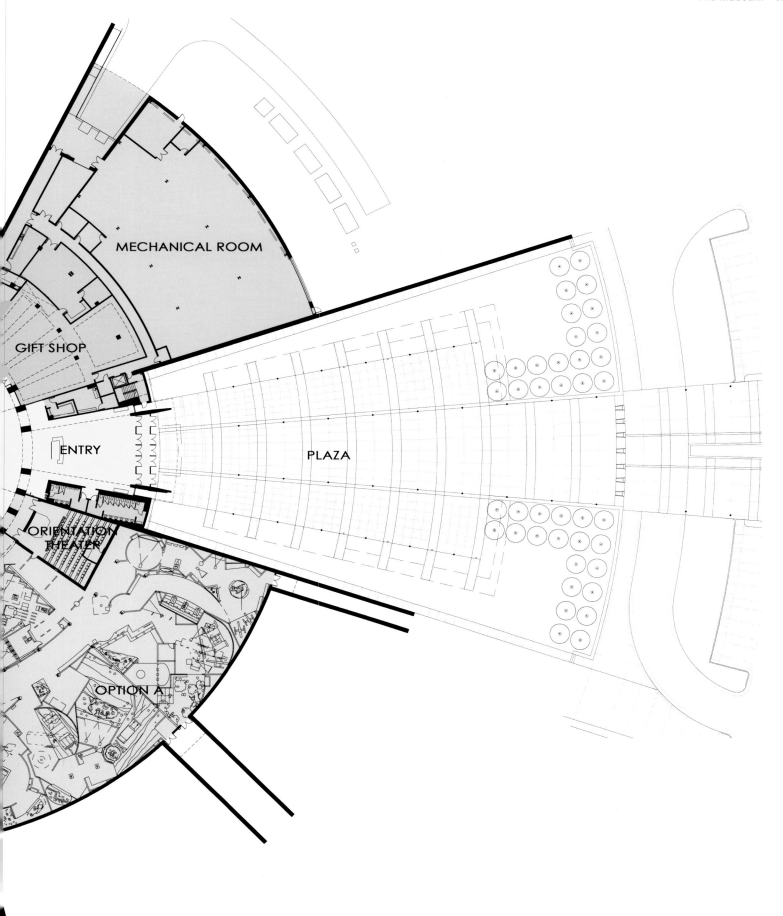

MECHANICAL ROOM

GIFT SHOP

ENTRY

PLAZA

ORIENTATION
THEATER

OPTION A

Leatherneck Gallery includes displays of Marines and their equipment, honoring the individual Marine. This is a central theme of both the organization and form of the building.

The perimeter of the circular atrium is formed by 38 concrete columns that support a concrete ring beam 45 feet above ground. The mast, which tapers in section from about 15 feet by 7 feet at the base to 4 feet by 3.5 feet at the top, rises through the center of the space at a 60-degree angle.

The 150-foot-diameter gallery contains Marine
aircraft, amphibious vehicles, and other large
exhibits of the Marine Corps' air, ground, and
sea forces.

AFEST PLACE IN KOREA WAS RIGHT BEHIND A
N OF MARINES. LORD, HOW THEY COULD FIGHT"

MAJOR GENERAL FRANK E. LOWE, U.S. ARMY

BUT WHAT I THINK OF A MAN WHO WANTS TO
RE, NOT LESS, A MAN YOU HAVE TO HOLD BACK, NOT SHOVE"

PRESIDENT LYNDON B. JOHNSON

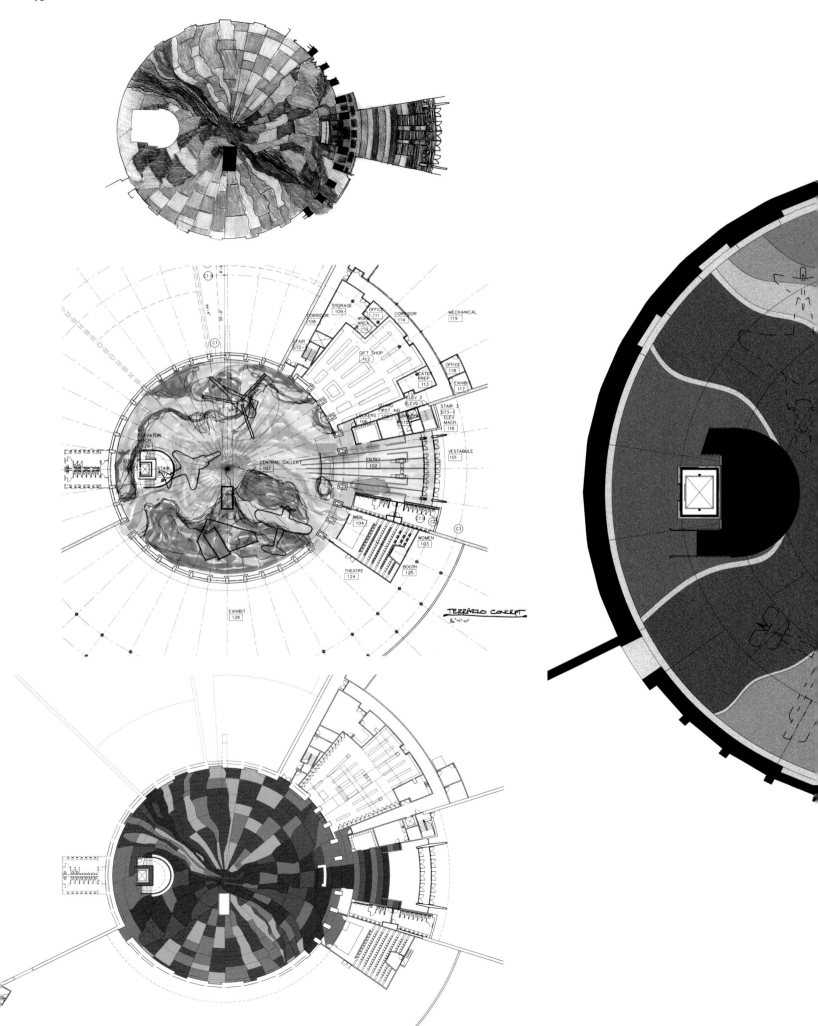

TERRAZZO CONCEPT
1/16"=1'-0"

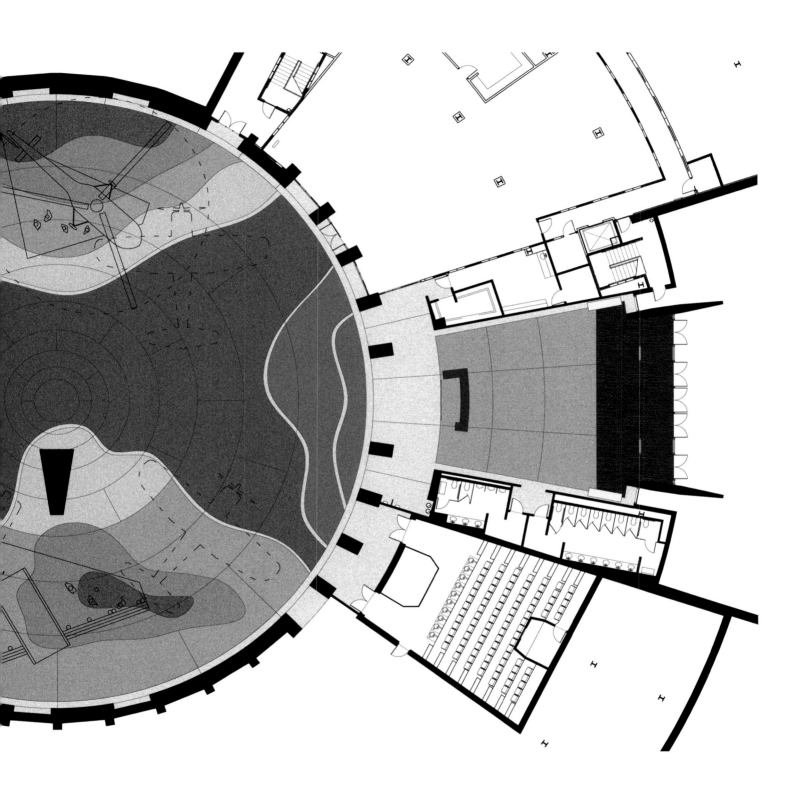

The Earth's varied surfaces, the domain
of Marines, inspired the floor pattern of
Leatherneck Gallery.

Skilled craftsmen worked with terrazzo to
create the finely detailed pattern.

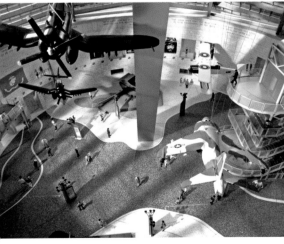

While the design began as a more literal
translation, it evolved into an abstract backdrop
that is appropriate to each of the three large floor
exhibits displayed in this space.

10

102

A ship's tower inspired the central stair, which comprises an observation deck and encloses an elevator core. Several models were built to explore every detail, from the stair treads to the handrails and even the core's exoskeleton.

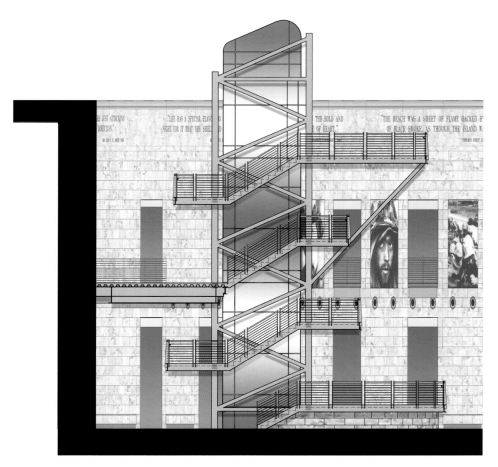

...O...MACHINE BUT WHAT I THINK OF A MAN WHO WANT...
...MORE, NOT LESS; A MAN YOU HAVE TO HOLD BACK, NOT SHOVE...

PRESIDENT LYNDON B. JOHNSO...

104

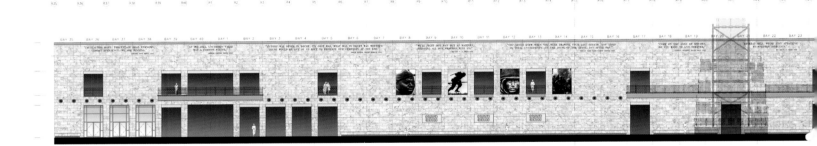

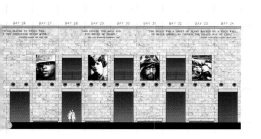

Leatherneck Gallery provides direct and
efficient access to an orientation theater and
40,000 square feet of exhibit space, as well
as to the Museum Store.

From the Central Gallery, visitors are encouraged to enter the Orientation Theater for a dynamic and educational introduction to the Marine Corps.

The theater exits onto the beginning of Legacy Walk, a fast track through the Museum. The first two galleries are the Making Marines exhibit, also known as the "Boot Camp Experience," and the changing gallery space, shown with a photography exhibit called The Global War on Terror.

1946–1953

SEND IN THE MARINES

THE MARINES SUSTAINED more than twice as many casualties in the Korean War as they did in France in World War I.

Politicians termed Korea a "Police Action," and historians called it "The Forgotten War," yet the conflict in Korea was as violent a war as the Marines ever fought. For three bloody years the United States and its allies battled against North Korea and China. At stake was the freedom of the Republic of Korea.

The U.S. Marine Corps, overlooked during the post-World War II focus on nuclear warfare, fought in Korea with traditional readiness and renewed intensity. Facing tenacious enemies, the Leathernecks distinguished themselves defending Pusan, assaulting Inchon, recapturing Seoul, breaking out of the Chosin Reservoir ("Frozen Chosin"), and holding the line during two years of stalemate. Along the way the Marines pioneered the tactical use of helicopters and refined sea-based close air support. The ravaged Republic of Korea survived and later flourished.

1946–1953

IN THE AIR, ON LAND AND SEA

1954–1975

1954–1975
IN THE AIR, ON LAND AND SEA

Legacy Walk is a timeline tracing American
and world history in parallel to Marine history.
It helps establish context for the non-Marine
audience and entices visitors into the galleries
to learn more.

114

Immersion galleries demonstrate to visitors what it was like to be a Marine in different eras. The Vietnam room, for instance, is hot and humid like the jungle. The Korea room is cold, just as it was in the months after the Marine landing at Inchon in 1950. Visitors see the sights, hear the sounds, and perhaps even smell some of the odors Marines experienced in different battle settings.

116

Opposite, top and bottom: Experiential exhibitory is coupled with dioramas, and auditory experiences are paired with visual, all in an attempt to connect with each museum visitor on an accessible and individual level.

Below: The Museum Store exudes Marine Corps spirit as it offers museum-goers a host of souvenirs.

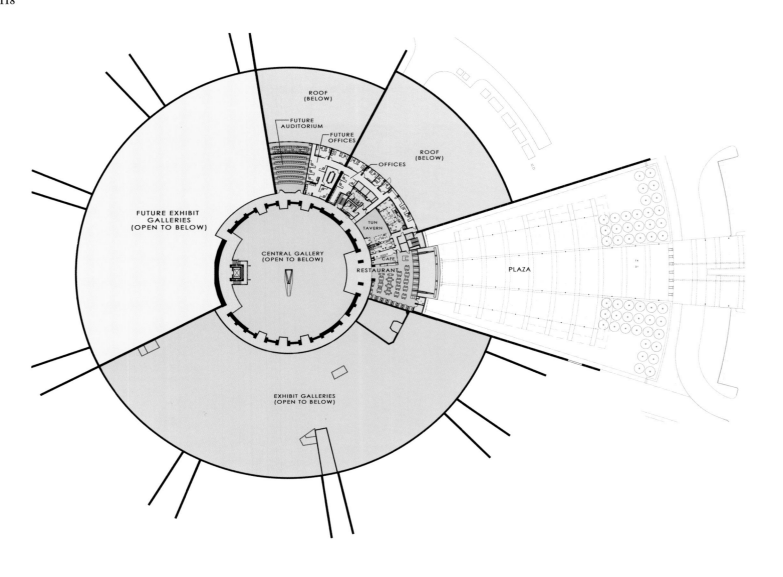

ROOF
(BELOW)

FUTURE
AUDITORIUM

FUTURE
OFFICES

OFFICES

ROOF
(BELOW)

FUTURE EXHIBIT
GALLERIES
(OPEN TO BELOW)

CENTRAL GALLERY
(OPEN TO BELOW)

TUN
TAVERN

CAFE

RESTAURANT

PLAZA

EXHIBIT GALLERIES
(OPEN TO BELOW)

Meeting and classroom spaces for Marine, community, and fraternal organizations are located on the second deck. Administrative offices and the two food service facilities are also located on this level. Tun Tavern is a recreation of the 18th-century public tavern in Philadelphia in which, according to legend, the first Colonial Marines were recruited by Captain Samuel Nicholas.

Located next door to Tun Tavern is the Mess Hall, a cafeteria-style facility with seating for up to 150 and menu offerings for breakfast and lunch.

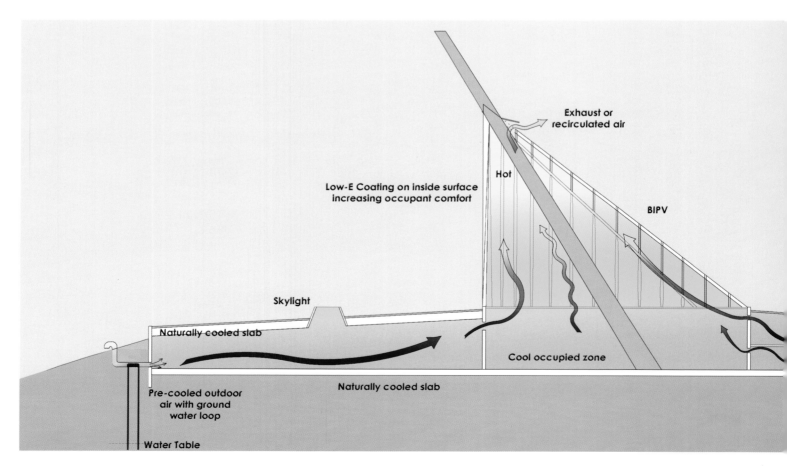

Exhaust or
recirculated air

Low-E Coating on inside surface
increasing occupant comfort

Hot

BIPV

Skylight

Naturally cooled slab

Cool occupied zone

Pre-cooled outdoor
air with ground
water loop

Naturally cooled slab

Water Table

Immersion of much of the museum into the site's hillside allows for an effective horizontal structure, which enhances pedestrian circulation. Berms and the green roofing over significant portions of the building also evoke the taking of the hill on Iwo Jima.

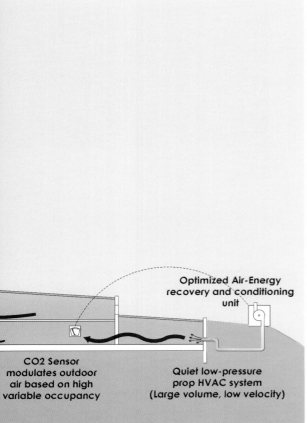

Optimized Air-Energy recovery and conditioning unit

CO2 Sensor modulates outdoor air based on high variable occupancy

Quiet low-pressure prop HVAC system (Large volume, low velocity)

A green roof is an extension of a roof system, which includes a special root-repelling membrane, a drainage system, a lightweight growing medium, and plants. Green roofs provide insulating benefits, aesthetic appeal, and require lower maintenance than standard roofs. This roof design, along with implementation of other sustainable "green" design features, provides for a responsible

building that is energy efficient, reducing
by approximately 30 percent the long-term
operating costs for the facility. Earth
integration of the building also helps evoke a
bunker-like image and leaves the lush foliage
of the 135-acre site intact. The building's
sustainable design features contribute
to a building that is easy to maintain
and physically secure.

The exterior's design and materials are designed to be simple and modest in appearance. The overall dramatic composition, particularly the upswept point of the soaring mast, creates a poised image of strength and stability—effectively interpreting the spirit of the Marine Corps.

07:

ENTRANCE
"THE MARINES WILL NEVER DISAPPOINT THE EXPECTATIONS OF THEIR COUNTRY - NEVER!"
MARINES

The Skylight

VISUAL imagery evoked by the skylight brings this iconic structure to life. It is a carefully orchestrated marriage between steel and glass, angles and planes, light and shadow. The skylight's primary element is a 210-foot-tall stainless-steel mast, which represents more than the flag raising at Iwo Jima. Canted at a 60-degree angle, it calls to mind myriad images. It is a drawn steel sword at its apogee, truly representative of *Man and Steel*—a concept at the heart of the Marine Corps. It is a Harrier jet at take-off, a Howitzer poised for fire, a makeshift cover replete with netting and support, and so much more. Just like great abstract art—the meaning, intent, and purpose reside in the eye of the beholder.

The skylight imbues a calm, contemplative aura. It also augments the other elements comprising Leatherneck Gallery. The observation structure and the balconies, both inspired by battleship functionality, extend the use of steel into the body of the space. Meanwhile, stone-clad walls and the globe-patterned terrazzo flooring contrast nicely with the steel elements, warming the space and instilling it with a timeless quality.

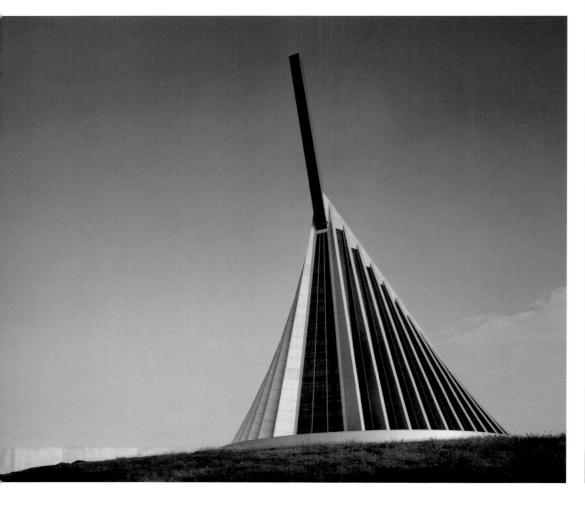

The most dramatic element of the Museum's
architecture is the 160-foot-tall skylight,
which is the ceiling of Leatherneck Gallery.
A 210-foot-tall stainless-steel-clad mast
bisects this skylight.

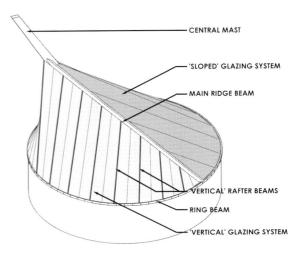

CENTRAL MAST

'SLOPED' GLAZING SYSTEM

MAIN RIDGE BEAM

'VERTICAL' RAFTER BEAMS

RING BEAM

'VERTICAL' GLAZING SYSTEM

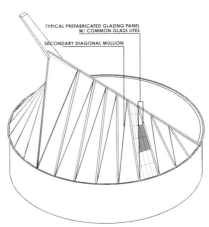

TYPICAL PREFABRICATED GLAZING PANEL
W/ COMMON GLASS LITES

SECONDARY DIAGONAL MULLION

VERTICAL GLAZING SYSTEM-OPTION B - AXON

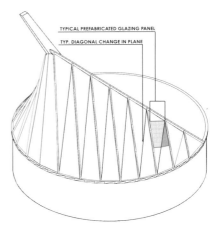

TYPICAL PREFABRICATED GLAZING PANEL

TYP. DIAGONAL CHANGE IN PLANE

VERTICAL GLAZING SYSTEM-OPTION A - AXON

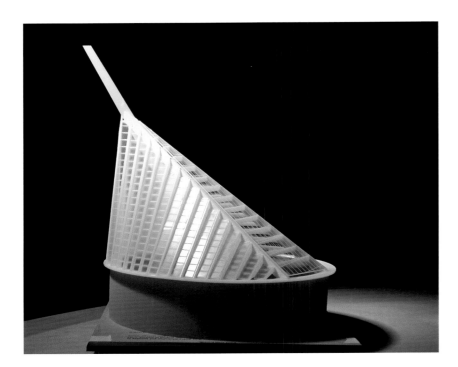

The original concept derived during the competition phase—to use triangular pieces of glass in varying sizes—would have been expensive and time-consuming to construct. Fentress Architects reviewed several different solutions and ultimately recommended the use of identical panes of rectangular glass to glaze the atrium. Mass production of identical objects, such as brick (and, in this instance, a pane of glass) significantly reduces costs.

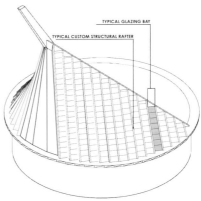

TYPICAL GLAZING BAY

TYPICAL CUSTOM STRUCTURAL RAFTER

VERTICAL GLAZING SYSTEM-OPTION C - AXON

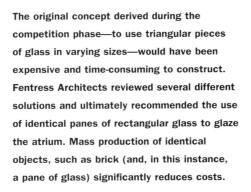

A wind tunnel test was used to define the structural engineering criteria to which the building would be designed. In addition to a 1:200 scale plastic model of the Museum form, replicas of the surrounding buildings and terrain features within a 900-foot radius were also made. The replicas and Museum form were covered with 522 pressure taps, or gauges that measure wind force, and placed on a turntable centered in the wind tunnel. Wind forces of up to 125 miles per hour were exerted and measurements were recorded as the turntable was rotated in 36 increments, or every 10 degrees. The data resulting from this and other tests produced a very functional and economical skylight.

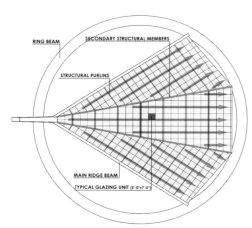

SLOPED GLAZING SYSTEM-OPTION B - ROOF PLAN

A mock-up of the skylight was used during the early construction phase, to test static and dynamic infiltration of air and water. This dynamic test is performed by simultaneous application of wind and water. The wind is typically simulated by positioning an aircraft propeller engine so that the wind it generates forces the water onto the mock-up surfaces. Simultaneously, differential pressure is added by use of the sealed chamber that causes the surface to deflect inward, creating the effect that simulates conditions of a wind-driven storm.

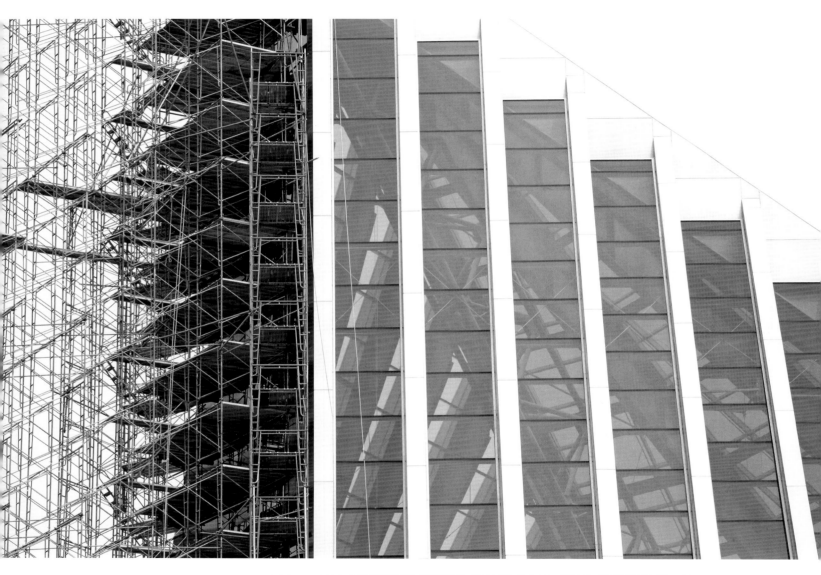

The skylight is framed by a system of custom
built-up steel members, called ridge and rib
beams. These members span from the ring
beam and connect to the mast and to each
other. Spanning between the first and second
beams and the fourth and fifth beams are
cable braces that create a triangular truss.
The braces follow the lines of mullions that
hold in place the skylight's 35,000 square
feet of glass. The rib and ridge beams are clad
in a system of aluminum panels.

The spire is 210 feet in length, rising from the 17,000-square-foot circular Central Gallery. From near the top of the spire, a glass curtain drops to the 40-foot-high wall of the Central Gallery.

144

The mast is framed along its length by a
triangular truss and anchored to a 20- by 20-
foot concrete mat foundation. It was designed
as a hollow triangular spire not only because
of weight concerns, but also because the
interior is used for maintenance access.

RT FO GROUND TROOPS AS PRO
ANNO BE MEASURED IN WORDS.
LIEUTE GENERAL ROBERT L. EICHELBERGER, US ARMY

Steel, with its flexibility, efficiency, and value, was elemental to the creation of the Museum's keystone feature, the 150-foot-diameter skylight, a conically shaped steel frame that creates the ceiling plane for the Central Gallery. The skylight, along with the aircraft suspended from its structural members, weighs 450 tons.

In addition to being the anchoring symbol of the building, the glass atrium affords a connection between indoor spaces and the outdoor environment through the introduction of sunlight and views into the occupied areas of the building.

"THE MARINES WILL NEVER
EXPECTATIONS OF THEIR C

"THE M
THE

4160

MARINES
127834

The mast is a stainless-steel-clad structural box beam, a strong feature that sparkles in the sunlight and is highlighted in dramatic fashion with exterior lighting at night.

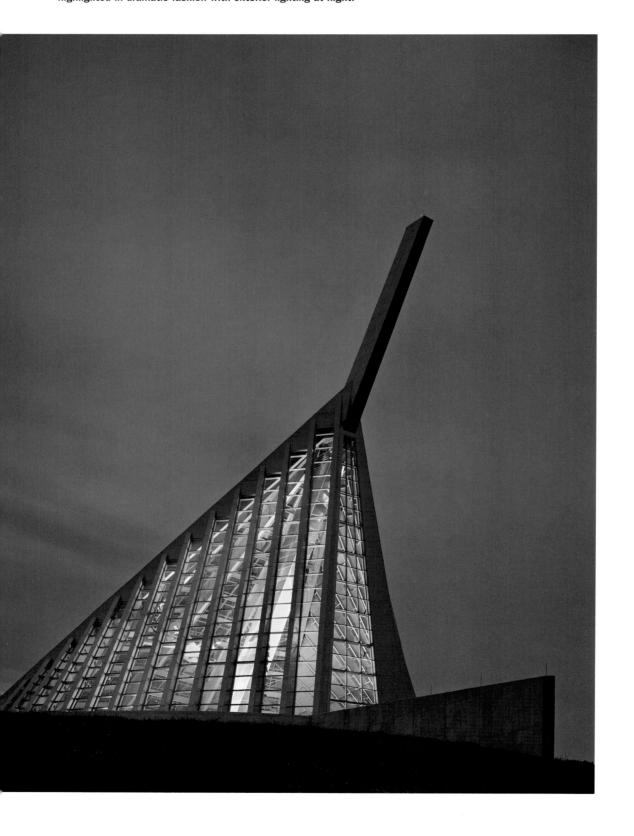

08:

REMAINING

portions of the site are preserved for the Semper Fidelis Memorial Park, demonstration grounds, other outdoor recreational offerings, a conference center, hotel, and archive facilities. The park incorporates outdoor sculptural features, inviting visitors to pay homage to and reflect upon the many contributions of the United States Marine Corps, made especially poignant through unit memorials and an area where the names of every U.S. Marine killed in the line of duty or missing in action will be inscribed. The park houses a chapel that will accommodate about 60 people at a time, its primary function being to serve as a place of personal prayer, reflection, and meditation.

Adjunct Spaces

The first phase of Semper Fidelis Memorial
Park culminates with a rallying point on which
one of the most famous Marine Corps mantras
is inscribed.

Flanking the Museum are the 10-acre Semper Fidelis Memorial Park to the south and a 2.3-acre outdoor lighted Parade Deck to the north. The Deck is where visitors can experience the excitement and pageantry of military parades, presentations of colors, Marine Band concerts, and other events. The Deck can also accommodate demonstrations of Marine helicopters, amphibious vehicles, and more.

Further out, yet still on axis, are an on-site hotel and conference center, as well as an office building that houses the Marine Corps History and Museums Division. This Division is charged with curatorial oversight of historic artifacts and collections. Adjacent facilities would include buildings for artifact restoration and preservation, as well as auxiliary buildings with office and meeting spaces for Marine Corps fraternal organizations.

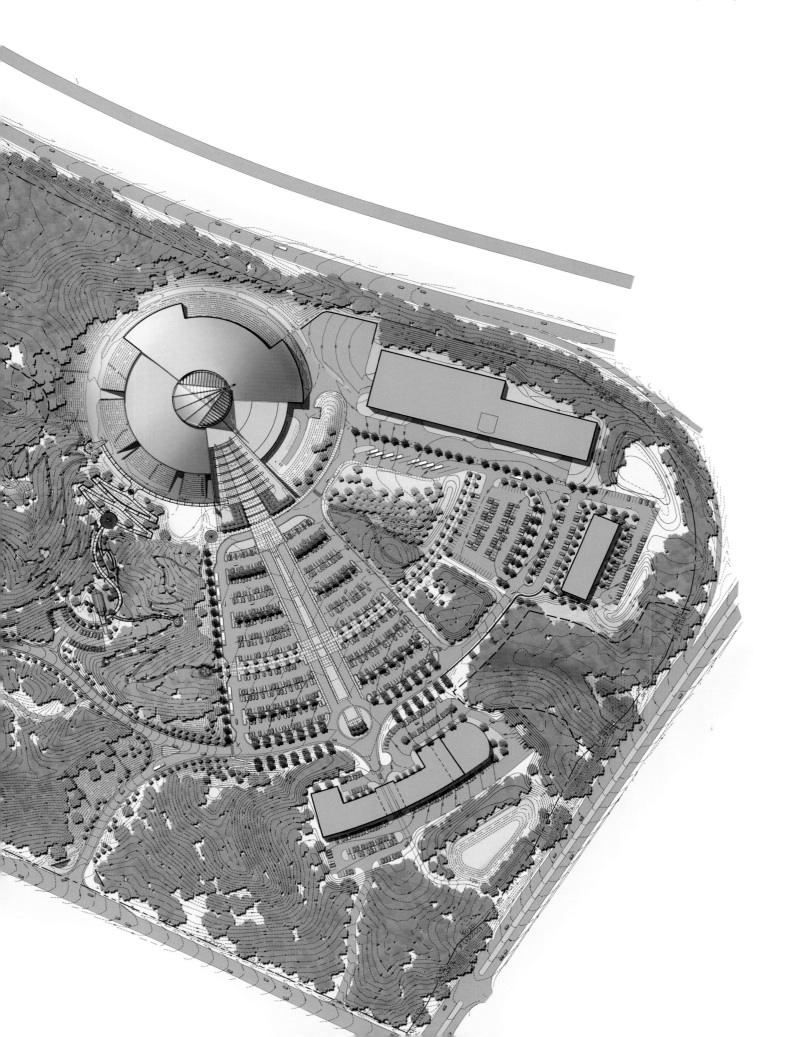

The first phase of Semper Fidelis Memorial
Park, which consists of three rallying points,
two statues (Iron Mike and Lejeune), and
paved walkways, opened in concert with the
Museum.

Quantico's Iron Mike, officially titled *Crusading for the Right*, depicts a World War I Marine holding a 1903 Springfield rifle and wearing a pack with a bayonet. The sculpture was commissioned by U.S. Army General John J. Pershing to commemorate the service of the U.S. Army's "doughboys." However, the sculptor inadvertently used a Marine private as a model and thereby included the Eagle, Globe, and Anchor insignia from his helmet. Since the artist would not remove the insignia, the Army refused to purchase the statue. It was then bought by Marine Corps General Smedley Butler, after he raised the funds needed, and it was installed at Headquarters on Marine Corps Base Quantico, Virginia circa 1920. With the opening of the Museum, it was relocated and now marks the entrance to Semper Fidelis Memorial Park.

The winding paved paths and rallying points provide excellent view corridors to the Museum's majestic mast. These paths and rallying points are lined with engraved bricks, which affirm for posterity individuals' Esprit de Corps.

164

A statue in honor of the 13th Commandant and Commanding General of the 2nd Army Division in World War I, MajGen John A. Lejeune, rises on the second rallying point.

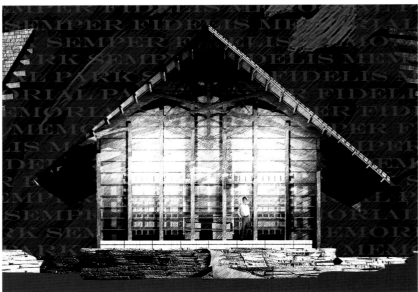

The Park's Chapel Phase results in the creation of a non-denominational, intimate gathering space atop a hill visible from the Museum. A water feature originates at the chapel to contribute to the visitor's experience of tranquility. The water begins as a trickling stream and gradually gains strength as it passes through a water wall and culminates in a large pool on the site's lower ground.

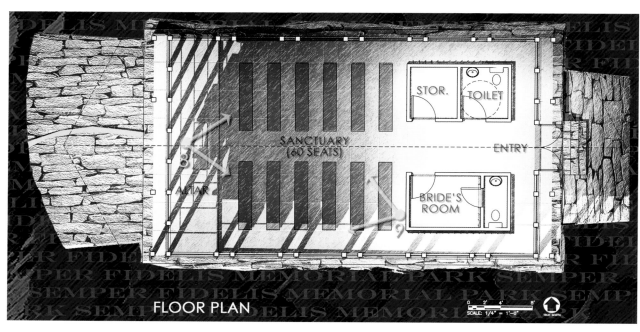

FLOOR PLAN

SANCTUARY
(60 SEATS)

ALTAR

STOR.

TOILET

ENTRY

BRIDE'S
ROOM

SCALE: 1/4" = 1'-0"

On the interior of the chapel, textured wood
planks, exposed wood beams, and walls of
glass allow museum visitors to fully appreciate
the surrounding natural environment.
Col Joseph Long, project manager for the
Marine Corps, described this concept as
a "transparent chapel in the woods."

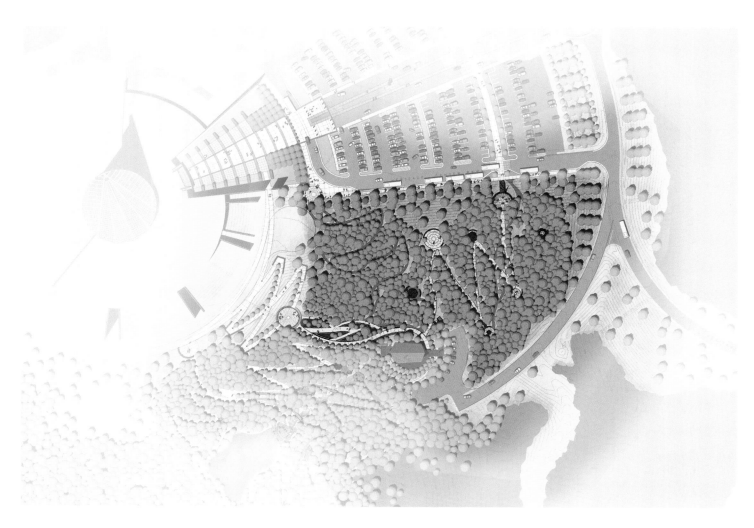

The Eastward and Westward Expansion Phases of the Park extend the bold, geometric, and formal landscape gestures—symbolic of the Marine Corps service at sea—as well as the informal interwoven paths, memorial walls, and additional rallying points that are evocative of the honor, courage, and commitment of the Marine Corps. Additional paved and decomposed granite walkways meander through these areas to provide for quiet reflection and discovery. They are lined with statues, plaques, and memorials to honor individual Marine units.

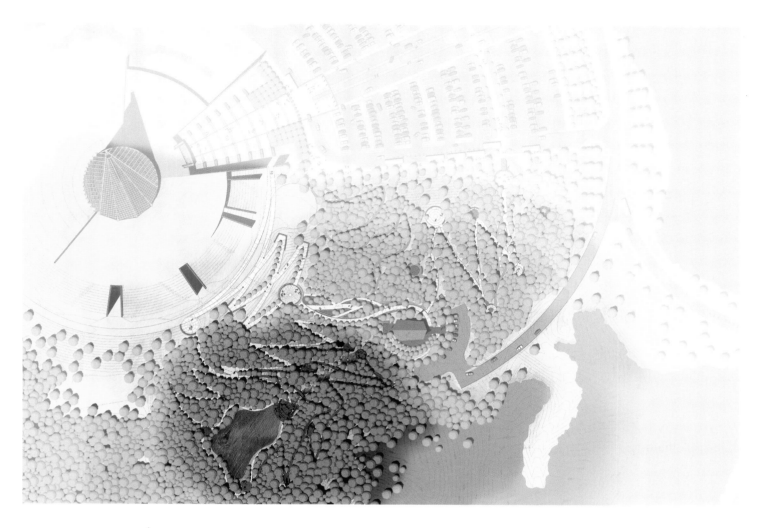

09:

THE Marine Corps takes pride in formally recording and documenting its history. Since 1775, a special unit—the Marine Corps Museum Division—has been officially dedicated to this purpose. The Division routinely dispatches field historians, combat artists, film makers, and photographers to record wherever and whenever history is being made.

Accomplishments

Brigadier General Gerald L. McKay, USMC (Ret)

Over time, the commitment to disciplined record keeping has resulted in an accumulation of a veritable treasure trove of documents, archives, artwork, and other material. Items of significance in the official Marine Corps repository include a library of 40,000 volumes on general military history, Marine history, and amphibious warfare; an archive of the operational records of the Corps; biographical, geographic, and unit histories; an oral history collection; and specialized collections of military music, combat art, and still photography.

176

"In essence, this is a museum that will set the bar for all other military museums in the future."

—MajGen Donald R. Gardner (Ret) President of the University of the Marine Corps *The Washington Times* November 9, 2006

The Marine Corps aggregated its world-class collection, including artifacts and weaponry, in a series of small museums on Marine Corps bases and similar facilities. That is, until the National Museum of the Marine Corps opened.

The rationale for creating a National Museum of the Marine Corps was that practical realities intruded on the Marine Corps' ability to properly preserve, store, and curate this increasingly important collection. Recall that the Marine Corps is the nation's premier war fighting force—"the tip of the spear" in Marine parlance. As such, vital national priorities would periodically take precedence over historical concerns, resulting in budgetary and similar restrictions. An immediate consequence was the inadequate storage and preservation of the collection.

Progressive deterioration of many items, some of iconic stature, increasingly concerned the Marine Corps' leadership and members of its community with interests in military history and scholarship. A sense of determination began to emerge. The collection, including irreplaceable items of national historic importance, such as the battle flag flown atop Mt. Suribachi on Iwo Jima during World War II, deserved proper preservation, storage, study, and display. Equally, a sense arose that the public might wish to learn about and better understand the historic actions of the Marine Corps—actions always taken for the benefit of the American people.

In the 1980s, the United States Congress authorized each of the military service branches to create museums documenting their service histories. The Marine Corps was the first branch to complete this undertaking.

This combination of circumstances led to a convergence of interest around the creation of the National Museum of the Marine Corps. Multiple objectives related to collection management, display, and the raising of public awareness about the historic role of the Marine Corps in our nation's defense were identified as worthy of further exploration.

"When we're done, we'll have raised close to $100 million for the whole project. We've been on schedule the whole time."

—Col John Ripley, United States
Marine Corps (Ret)
Former Director, USMC History
and Museums Division
April 9, 2007

Accomplishment 1:

Effective public–private agreement

Key to the project's success has been its governance structure, which is defined in a formal memorandum of understanding between the United States Marine Corps and the Marine Corps Heritage Foundation. The agreement defines roles and responsibilities of the parties both for the initial development phase and beyond.

Under the agreement, the Marine Corps funds early planning and design, while the Foundation funds construction. A key aspect of the agreement is the gifting of the Museum, including the building shell, to the Marine Corps upon completion.

The terms of the agreement stipulate that the Marine Corps, through its Museum Division, will operate the Museum, while the Foundation will operate revenue centers including the Museum store and restaurants.

Accomplishment 2:

A well-located site

The 135-acre parcel of land gifted by Prince William County surpassed initial projections of 400,000 visitors each year, when at six months the Museum welcomed more than 300,000 visitors.

Adjacency to Interstate 95 proved to be an excellent location for the Heritage Center. Fentress Architects not only located the Museum on the site's highest point, but also located it at a bend in the Interstate so that oncoming traffic in both directions is on axis with the Museum for a minute or more.

Accomplishment 3:

Enthusiastic donor response

More than $60 million in private donations have been secured toward construction of the first phase of the National Museum and Heritage Center. These funds came in amounts large and small from more than 80,000 individuals, corporations, foundations, and governmental entities, demonstrating a pluralistic appeal by both the Marine community and the general public.

A critical element of the original campaign's success was the early recruitment and involvement of a group of distinguished business leaders. These volunteers, known as the Founders, provided stewardship, guidance, and the philanthropic impetus essential to launching and maintaining a successful capital drive of this magnitude.

A special commemorative coin was released in 2005 by the U.S. Mint.

"We are the Marines. And in this museum, our story is told. It is a single, monumental story, made up of 231 years of many separate stories of heroism and courage, of dedication and sacrifice, of service to our country and to our corps, of honor and loyalty to each other in war and in peace."

—Jim Lehrer, author and PBS nightly news anchor

Accomplishment 4:
Dramatic architecture

The project also benefited considerably from the release of a commemorative coin by the United States Mint in 2005 marking the 230th anniversary of the Marine Corps. Surcharges from this release were allocated to the Museum's construction fund.

In the spring of 2007, with the first phase open, the Marine Corps and Marine Corps Heritage Foundation seamlessly launched campaigns to complete additional projects for the Museum and Heritage Center using the same public–private formula.

Project stakeholders made an early decision that the National Museum must be more than a mundane government building. Architecture was seen as a key means of delivering on the promise of a truly distinctive, world-class facility and visitor experience. Fentress Architects was selected to design the Museum following a national competition.

Fentress Architects' vision for the National Museum generated accolades from critics around the country. For the general public,

the most prominent visual association is with the flag raising at Iwo Jima, both through Joe Rosenthal's iconic photograph and the sculptural rendition at the Marine Corps War Memorial in Arlington, Virginia. For Marines, the building's angled main mast, rising even higher than the United States Capitol, also evokes other familiar imagery such as swords at salute and Howitzers raised to fire.

As the National Museum rose, it rapidly became a regional landmark—largely due to the strong thematic and emotional associations inherent in the architectural concept. The strength of its architecture has already, and will surely continue to be, a key element sustaining public awareness of the National Museum.

The Dunham Medal of Honor ceremony held in Leatherneck Gallery was just one of the more than 250 events held at the Museum during its first year of operation.

"There have been more than four million men and women who have worn the uniform of a United States Marine. This museum is about all of them ... That's because this museum is about what it means to be a Marine, no matter the time, the length, place, rank, or nature of the service."

—Jim Lehrer, author and PBS nightly news anchor

The National Museum of the Marine Corps welcomed more than 400,000 visitors during its first year of operation.

"Cultural critics across the nation are unanimously hailing the Museum for its integrity and technological innovation in telling the story of the Corps since our nation's founding."
—LtGen Ronald Christmas,
United States Marine
Corps (Ret)
President, Marine Corps
Heritage Foundation
January 12, 2007

Accomplishment 5:
Compelling exhibitory

As with the architecture, engaging exhibits were seen as another important element in ensuring an attractive, high-quality visitor experience for the museum. Christopher Chadbourne Associates developed exhibits that work well and are fully integrated with the building's architecture.

During the planning stage, members of Fentress Architects and Christopher Chadbourne Associates joined Museum Division staff on visits to museums, particularly those with military foci, to learn the best practices for creating cutting-edge facilities and maximizing the visitor experience.

The National Museum's exhibits were designed for scholars and laymen alike based on insights gained from these trips and Chadbourne's past experiences. State-of-the-art interactive techniques and computer technologies educate and inform visitors as well as sustain their interest. Exhibit displays bring to life many key artifacts.

Immersion galleries, which replicate a key event from each era, use climate control, realistic mannequins, and artifacts to convey Marine experiences to each visitor on an individual level.

"This new museum, I believe, will quickly become the barometer by which all other major contemporary American military and history museums will be measured."
—Dr. Lori Verderame,
certified art and antiques appraiser
January 20, 2007

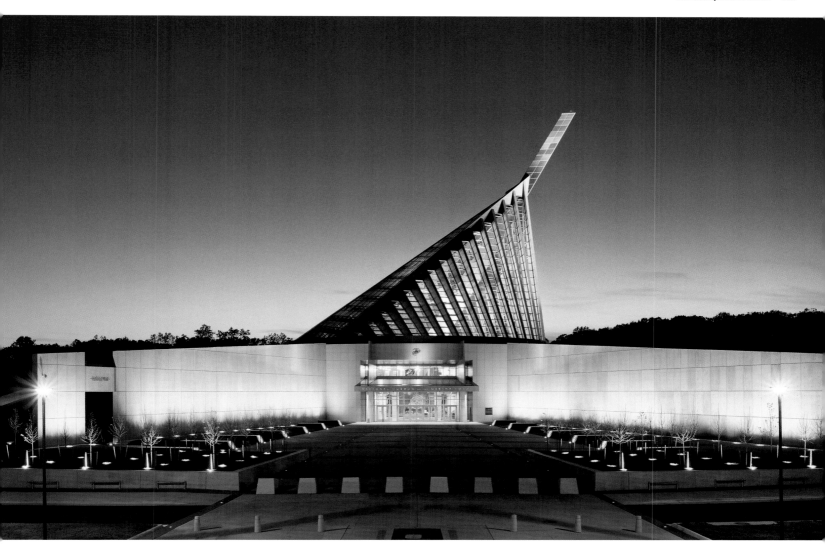

Future accomplishments

Construction of the National Museum, development of the Heritage Center site, and installation of the first set of exhibits represent key accomplishments from the project's initial development phase. Without doubt, future phases will realize similar success and the Heritage Center will continue to advance, just like its raison d'etre, the United States Marine Corps.

"The other architects had plans that were good, they looked worthy, but their designs looked like other museums. Curtis Worth Fentress, of Fentress Architects, had a vision that was so powerful, so perfect."

—Col John Ripley,
United States Marine Corps (Ret)
Former Director, USMC History and
Museums Division
April 9, 2007

Appendix

Timeline

Late 1980s	United States Congress appropriates funds for each branch of the armed forces to build a museum.
1995	The Marine Corps Historical Foundation further defined its project by publicly announcing its intention to create the Unites States Marine Corps Heritage Center.
1996–98	Research resulted in an agreement between the Marine Corps, the Department of the Navy, and the Marine Corps Heritage Foundation to make the Heritage Center a reality.
1999	The capital campaign was formally authorized for an $80-million Heritage Center and its first phase of development, the National Museum of the Marine Corps.
November 30, 2000	Engineering Field Activity (EFA) Chesapeake's Capt William F. Boudra, Commanding Officer, and Tess Manns, Project Manager, announced a two-stage, national design competition to select an architect for the Heritage Center.
July 9, 2001	Gen J.L. Jones ratified the selection of Fentress Architects and announced it as the winning design firm.
June 2003	The 14-foot-tall, 10-foot-wide and 20-foot-long interactive model was completed.
September 28, 2003	Groundbreaking ceremony held.
April 2004	Centex Construction selected as the general contractor
March 30, 2005	Three cranes, two capable of each lifting 250 tons, lifted the mast into place.
February 2006	Building fully enclosed.
November 10, 2006	National Museum of the Marine Corps opened by President George W. Bush.
July 8, 2007	Museum welcomes 400,000th visitor.

Materials and Design Features

Museum size

Phase I	120,000 square feet
Full build-out	214,000 square feet
Central Gallery	18,000 square feet

Exhibit space

(Phase I)	40,000 square feet
Surface parking	368 spaces
Heritage Center site	135 acres
Annual visitors	500,000 in 2007
Glass panels	½-inch, clear, low-iron glass
Cost	$42 million
Building	$30 million
Exhibits	$12 million

20,000	cubic yards of concrete
1,500	tons of rebar
1,300	tons of structural steel
$^2/_3$	acre of glass in the skylight
14	major aircraft on display
11	major ground vehicles on display
180	pounds of hard candy eaten by construction workers
720	gallons of coffee consumed by construction workers

Project Team Credits

Primary design and construction team credits

Fentress Bradburn Architects	Architect
Jacobs Facilities	Project management
Centex Construction	Contractor
Christopher Chadbourne & Associates Inc.	Exhibit designer

Fentress Architects

Key personnel

Curtis W. Fentress, Principal-in-Charge of Design

Brian Chaffee, Project Architect

Bob Louden, Project Manager

Charles Cannon, Job Captain

Scott Dergance, Chris Peters, John Stoltze, Sonny Willier

Additional team members

Robin Ault	David Pak	Lorenzo DeNinno
Mario Figueroa	Mark Wagner	Jason Knowles
Samantha Mangnall	Ron Booth	Adam Snodgrass
Tanya Troiano	Lisa Hillmer	Brad Wonnacott
Carey Ball	Marilyn White	Stephanie Leahey
Jennifer Fonseca	Tymmie Byram	Jim Sobey
Tracy Matteson	Hayden Hirschfeld	Kelly Wright
Denise Trujillo	Felipe Pineiro	Andrea Devitt
Greg Billingham	Nate James	Lauren Lee
Evan Gidez	Mike Rinken	Amy Solomon
David Mecham	Laura Wilhelm	Jason Epstein
Shawn Turney	Nathan Kibler-Silengo	Jennifer Linde-Wilson
James H. Bradburn	Robin Mae Schick	Derek Starkenburg
Karen Gilbert	Cash Wilson	Deborah Faris
Michael Nixon	Jayne Coburn	Jason Loui
William Vinyard	Ned Kirschbaum	Les Stuart
Todd Britton	Maria Simon	
Carl Goodiel	Jacqueline Wisniewski	

Consultants to Fentress Architects

Patton Harris Rust & Associates, PC	Civil engineer
Weidlinger Associates Inc.	Structural engineer
Hankins & Andersen Inc.	Mechanical, electrical, plumbing and fire protection
Architectural Energy Corporation	Sustainable design
studioINSITE, LLC	Landscape architect
Brandston Partnership Inc.	Lighting design
Shen Milsom & Wilke Inc.	Audio visual/acoustical
Carpenter Associates	Specifications consultant
Froehling & Robertson Inc.	Geotechnical consultant
Project Management Services Inc.	Cost consultant
Kohnen Construction Inc.	Cost consultant
USMC Col Joseph H. Alexander (Ret)	Historian
Thomas Ricca Associates Inc.	Food service
Cini-Little Inc.	Food service

Client Credits

Selection jury credits

Design jury: Hal Aber, Director of Design and Planning for the Smithsonian; Eric Van Aukee, Vice President of Perkins + Will; Gregory Hunt, Dean of Architecture for Catholic University; and Richard Logan, Vice President of Gensler.

Technical evaluation panel: Tracey Johnson and Tess Manns, both Navy architects, Engineering Facility Activity EFA Chesapeake; Bob Greco, Head of Civil and Structural Engineering for the Navy's EFA Chesapeake; LtCol Jon Hoffman, USMC Department Director for the Historical Division; and Col Gerald Thomas (Ret) from the USMC Heritage Foundation.

The selection board, headed by the USMC Heritage Foundation President, LtGen G.R. Christmas (Ret), included the following from the Department of the Navy EFA Chesapeake: Tony Diagonale, Head of Architecture; William Faught, Head of Planning; and Maggie Gervais, Head of Contracts. Also on the selection board, from the USMC Heritage Foundation, were Gen Joseph Went (Ret); Marshall Carter, Founder; and Col John Ripley (Ret), Director of The Marine Corps History & Museums Division.

Ex-officio participant-at-large: Col Joseph Long, Marine Corps Project Manager

Marine Corps Heritage Foundation

LtGen Ronald Christmas, USMC (Ret)
President, Marine Corps Heritage Foundation

BrigGen Gerald L. McKay, USMC (Ret)
Chief Operating Officer, Marine Corps Heritage Foundation

Col Raymond A. Hord, USMC (Ret)
Vice President of Development and Marketing, Marine Corps Heritage Foundation

Susan L. Hodges
Vice President of Administration and Finance, Marine Corps Heritage Foundation

United States Marine Corps

Commandants: Gen Chuck Krulak, Gen James Jones, and Gen Michael Hagee

Assistant Commandants of the Marine Corps (and chairmen of the Marine Corps Heritage Center Executive Steering Committee): Gen Terrance Dake, Gen Mike Williams, and Gen William Nyland

Marine Corps Legislative Affairs: Director, MajGen Tony Corwin

Marine Corps Legal Counsel: Peter Murphy, Robert Hogue, LtCol Craig Jensen, and Penny Clark

Marine Corps Resources and Finance: Lee Dixon and Charles Cook

Marine Corps Installations and Facilities: Paul Hubbell, Jane Brattain, and Chuck Rushing

Marine Corps History and Museums Division: Director, Col John Ripley (Ret); Deputy Director, Col Jon Hoffman

Marine Corps Heritage Center Program Manager: Col Joseph Long

NAVFAC Washington/Engineering Field Activity Chesapeake

CAPT William Boudra CEC, USN; CAPT Tom Calhoun CEC, USN

CAPT Chris Mossey, CEC, USN; CAPT Kevin Slates, CEC, USN

IPT Leaders: LCDR Brian Moore, CEC, USN; LCDR Mark Edelson, CEC, USN; CDR Ben Pina, CEC, USN; CDR Clayton Mitchell, CEC, USN

Senior Architect: Anthony Diagonale

Project Architect: Tess Manns

Project Engineer: Jason Root

Activity Operations Director: Robert A. Greco

Acquisition: Maggie Gervais

Counsel: Cindy Guill

Design Competition Wins

Since 1980, Fentress Architects has been awarded the following 28 major national and international project commissions through design competitions.

University of California – Irvine Humanities Building, Irvine, California, 2007

San Joaquin County Administration Building, Stockton, California, 2007

Santa Fe Civic Center, Santa Fe, New Mexico, 2005

Dubai Mixed Use Towers, United Arab Emirates, 2004

New FBI Office Building, Location Confidential, 2003

Cape Girardeau Federal Courthouse, Cape Girardeau, Missouri, 2003

National Museum of the Marine Corps, Quantico, Virginia, 2001

Larimer County Courthouse Offices, Fort Collins, Colorado, 2000

Loveland Police and Courts Building, Loveland, Colorado, 1999

3790 Howard Hughes Parkway, Las Vegas, Nevada, 1998

3993 Howard Hughes Parkway, Las Vegas, Nevada, 1998

Civic Center Parking Structure, Fort Collins, Colorado, 1998

Gulf Canada Resources, Ltd., Denver, Colorado, 1996

Bentley Ratkovich–The Pike Project, Long Beach, California, 1996

Doha International Airport, Doha, Qatar, 1996

Larimer County Justice Center, Fort Collins, Colorado, 1996

Hughes Center Office Tower, Las Vegas, Nevada, 1995

City of Oakland Administration Buildings, Oakland, California, 1995

United States Postal Service Processing and Distribution Center, Anaheim, California, 1994

Incheon International Airport, Seoul, Korea, 1993

Avon Recreation Center, Avon, Colorado, 1993

Clark County Government Center, Las Vegas, Nevada, 1992

National Cowboy and Western Heritage Museum, Oklahoma City, Oklahoma, 1992

National Museum of Wildlife Art, Jackson, Wyoming, 1991

United States Postal Service Vehicle Maintenance Facility, Seattle, Washington, 1990

Natural Resources Building, Olympia, Washington, 1989

Colorado Convention Center, Denver, Colorado, 1987

Data General Plant, Fountain, Colorado, 1986

Photo Credits

Nick Merrick © Hedrich Blessing
Pages 8, 14, 17, 65, 67(right), 83(below), 86, 91, 95, 101, 106(left), 110, 120, 123, 127, 130, 132, 133, 141, 143, 145, 146(above), 150, 152, 153

Carl Dalio
Pages 82, 90(right), 94(above)

© Ron Johnson
Pages 52, 53, 58(below), 59, 128, 134(left), 148(below)

Jason Knowles © Fentress Architects
Pages 58(above), 60, 61, 83(above), 99(below left), 125, 126(left), 135, 136(below center, right), 137, 138(above), 139, 140(right), 167

Curtis Worth Fentress
Pages 49, 50

© Fentress Architects
Pages 18, 19, 20, 24–31, 41–45, 51, 54, 55, 62(below), 63, 66, 67(left), 70(above), 72(below), 74(below), 75, 78(above, below right), 80, 81, 84, 88, 89, 90(left), 92, 93, 94 (below), 96, 97, 98(above), 99 (above and below right), 102, 104, 106(right), 108(above), 113(above), 114(below), 115, 118, 119, 122, 124, 136(above), 138(below), 140(left), 142, 144, 146(below), 147 (below), 148(above), 156–160, 162(below), 165, 166, 168, 169, 170(above), 171(above)

Courtesy of Department of the Navy
Pages 32–37

Courtesy of United States Marine Corps and Marine Corps Heritage Foundation
Pages 68, 69, 70(below), 71, 72(above), 73, 78(below left), 112, 126(right), 178, 179

Christopher Chadbourne Associates
Page 114(above)

In-Site Design Group Inc.
Pages 162(above), 164, 170(below), 171(below)

Weidlinger Associates Inc.
Pages 134(right), 136(below left)

James P. Scholz
Pages 38, 74(above), 76, 79, 85, 100, 103, 105, 107(below), 108(below), 109, 116, 117, 129, 149, 155, 163, 172, 181

Tim Sloan/AFP/Getty Images
Pages 46, 62(above)

Tim Graham/Tim Graham Photo Library/Getty Images
Page 56

Robert Nickelsberg/ Getty Images
Page 57

Chip Somodevilla/Getty Images News
Pages 107(above), 114(below), 161, 174

AP/World Wide Photos
Page 48

Acknowledgments

Just like its muse—the National Museum of the Marine Corps—
this monograph was a collaborative effort. Not only is the book a
collection of essays, it is also the product of diligent efforts made
by so many talented and dedicated individuals.

Thank you to the essayists: General Michael W. Hagee, Colonel
Joseph H. Alexander (Ret), Lieutenant General Ronald Christmas,
Colonel Joseph C. Long (Ret), Curtis Worth Fentress, and
Brigadier General Gerald L. McKay.

Thank you to the project and client teams credited in the Appendix.

Thank you to the monograph team of researchers and reviewers:
Karen Gilbert, Jennifer Fonseca, Karen Bomar, Carol Carr, Wendy
Gossett, Jason Knowles, Tymmie Byram, and Diana Blevins.

Thank you to the dedicated team at The Images Publishing Group:
Paul Latham, Alessina Brooks, Robyn Beaver, Rod Gilbert, and
Jason Phillips.

It has been an honor and privilege to work on *Portal to the Corps*. In
the last ten years of writing about architecture, I have never been so
moved by a client and their mission. The United States Marine
Corps and Marine Corps Heritage Foundation have educated me,
inspired me, and made me even more proud to be an American.

Jessica del Pilar, Editor